MOUNTAIN BIKES

MAINTAINING, REPAIRING & UPGRADING

MOUNTAIN BIKES

MAINTAINING, REPAIRING & UPGRADING

Herman Seidl

 Sterling Publishing Co., Inc.   New York

Library of Congress Cataloging-in-Publication Data

Seidl, Herman.
  [Mountain-Bike-Technik. English]
  Mountain bikes : maintaining, repairing, and upgrading / by Herman
Seidl.
      p.   cm.
  Includes index.
  ISBN 0-8069-8764-2
  1. All terrain bicycles—Maintenance and repair.   2. All terrain
bicycles.   3. All terrain cycling.   I. Title.
TL430.S3713   1992
629.28'772—dc20   92-18773
                                                   CIP

Translated by Elisabeth E. Reinersmann

10   9   8   7   6   5   4   3   2

All photographs are by the author except: Campagnolo, 82; Wende Cragg, 14,
18(3), 20, 22(left); Kästle, 12, 78, 89, 98, 100; Koga Miyata, 50; Maroné, 41(m);
Mountain Cycles, 103; Carlo de Pisis, 63; Riff-Raff, 26; Schwinn, 16/17; Trek,
10, 13, 52, 77; Peter Witek, 67, 69, 74

First paperback edition published in 1993 by
Sterling Publishing Company, Inc.
387 Park Avenue South, New York, N.Y. 10016
English translation © 1992 by Sterling Publishing Company, Inc.
Originally published Germany by BLV Verlagsgesellschaft mbH
under the title *Mountain-Bike Technik*
© 1991 by BLV Verlagsgesellschaft mbH, München Wien Zürich
Distributed in Canada by Sterling Publishing
% Canadian Manda Group, P.O. Box 920, Station U
Toronto, Ontario, Canada M8Z 5P9
Distributed in Great Britain and Europe by Cassell PLC
Villiers House, 41/47 Strand, London WC2N 5JE, England
Distributed in Australia by Capricorn Link Ltd.
P.O. Box 665, Lane Cove, NSW 2066
Printed and bound in Hong Kong
All rights reserved

Sterling ISBN 0-8069-8764-2 Trade
              0-8069-8765-0 Paper

Preface

The mountain bike revolution of the 1980s is without parallel. Within one decade, as it took the world by storm, mountain biking became almost a spiritual movement. Bike riding is one of the most frugal and environmentally safe ways to travel from point A to point B.

A few biking "freaks" in California, having fun on their bikes on their day off, turned a hobby into a worldwide mass movement. A new type of bike cannot by itself account for such a boom; other factors had to be in place for this to happen. The mountain bike's rapid increase in popularity was influenced by social and economic situations, and by technical improvements that had the needs of the biker at heart. The introduction of the first mountain bike at a bike convention in Long Beach, California, early in the 1980s coincided with the need for a bike that combined technical superiority, ease of care, and multi-purpose use. In the beginning, individual private efforts fueled this development; now a whole industry is involved.

Technological advances come fast and furious, all committed to finding better solutions. While biking has become easier, making it possible for a biker to explore new terrain, the highly specialized bike has lost some of its simplicity. This book may provide some insight into a variety of technological aspects of this development.

Herman Seidl

Mountain biking combines the fascination of nature with the fascination of technology.

Contents

Introduction

The Bike: A Symbol of the Times

Many factors were responsible for the bike boom, and all came together at the right time. The "bike freaks" who had their fun at the "Repack" races had left the hectic inner cities and moved to Fairfax, a small town in Marin County, north of San Francisco. Here they found what could only be seen in advertisements—a life of freedom in a natural setting. The mountain bike, at the time still called the "clunker," gave them the means to enjoy what they'd found.

The Perfect Image

Over time, more and more people, tired of too much "civilization," joined the search for just such freedom. Coinciding with this development was a worldwide health consciousness of unprecedented proportions. Biologically sound nutrition and physical fitness became musts for concerned people in industrial nations, a post-industrial trend that sociologist Susan Sontag called an incessant materialization of the body-cult, with an "ideology of self-improvement" at its root.

The mountain bike represented a product for a positive hobby; it was the symbol of a successful mix of freedom, fitness, and improved technology. It allowed for almost unrestricted travel using "pedal power," and it was environmentally friendly. This was a perfect image, the stuff of an advertiser's dream. It's no wonder that biking (and specifically mountain biking) is used so often in commercials.

Intelligent Technology

Technical advances in the design and construction of mountain bikes played a significant role in this boom. The bike industry in the 1970s didn't spend much time improving its products. Following the trends of the time, research was almost totally concerned with the development of motor vehicles and racing bikes. Only a few people on the fringes thought about off-road biking. Yet, clever technicians and business people in Japan smelled a revolution in the making and business people in California were looking for inexpensive manufacturers. They went to Japan and (almost overnight) Japanese industry responded: Shimano, Suntour, Tange, and Araya surprised everyone with convincing, revolutionary technology, improved handling, beautiful design, and smart marketing. People in Japan thought seriously about a subject that was almost ignored in the age of the automobile: the bike.

The impetus for such developments came from Italy, the land of indoor bike racing, and of road racing. However, the Japanese took development and design much further. The quality of their bike technology was unequalled, and not only for racing bikes. They made bikes available to the masses; Japan became the unquestioned leader in the mountain bike industry. The Japanese aimed to make biking as comfortable as possible for the professional, as well as for the beginner.

The Mountain Bike Boom

Clever businessmen in the United States knew how to take advantage of the marketplace by producing a product cheaply in a foreign country, and then making it available in the U.S. at an affordable price. Frames and other accessories could be manufactured cheaply and in great numbers in Asia. The mountain bike, with its straight handlebars, was easier to handle, much smaller than the ordinary bike, more comfortable, displayed exciting technology, and (most important) it made a dream attainable—freedom to leave the paved streets and highways. It was a golden concept for success.

1986 will be remembered as the year of the mountain bike explosion. In the U.S., sales of bicycles increased by 80%, with the mountain bike taking a 35% share. It is estimated that in 1989, in the U.S., 7.5 million bikes were sold.

Women can't escape the magic of the mountain bike

The Trend Reaches Europe

Europe was slow to catch on to this trend; the age of the automobile was still in full bloom, the ecology movement still in its infancy. The bike industry was anything but modern and aggressive. The BMX (Bicycle Motor Cross) fad turned out to be brief and economically insignificant; the so-called "terrain" bike was clumsy, heavy, and, at best, a trendy, short-lived experiment.

The enormous mountain bike wave crashed over Europe, just like so many other trends imported from the U.S. Europe was ready for a technologically advanced, interesting bicycle, for the commuter as well as for the recreational biker. In addition, the "Old World" became socially aware. Within 14 years (1976–1990) the sales of new bicycles increased from 2.3 million to 4.5 million. The mountain bike was heavily involved in the increase in bike sales. In 1989 150,000 bikes were sold; in 1990 this number increased to 400,000. These statistics give a vivid picture of the rapid development within the bike industry, with mountain bikes accounting for almost all of the bikes that were imported.

This boom resulted in a renewal of the entire bike industry. Rapid growth and favorable predictions for the future turned the bike business into a gold mine. Every bike manufacturer has joined the game.

The "clunker" people who raced down fire trails in 1976 in Marin County on their 40-year-old bikes didn't have the slightest notion that such a trend was in the making.

Discovering the adventure of nature and freedom on a bike

Pioneers of a new era: Charles Kelly and Joe Breeze at Mineral King Mountain, California (1978), on their first self-made mountain bikes

History of the Mountain Bike

The history of the mountain bike is one of rapidly developing technology. In the mid-1970s a few biking "freaks" in California didn't just turn a hobby and a number of innovative technical improvements into a profession. With their "fat-tire" bikes they set in motion a worldwide biking boom.

Ignaz Schwinn

Ignaz Schwinn was born in Germany in 1860. After training as an engineer, he worked for a north German bicycle manufacturer. He was obsessed by the idea of building a better bike. However, his innovative ideas fell victim to tradition. Convinced that his ideas had merit, he immigrated to Chicago in 1891. Four years later, together with Adolf Arnold, he founded "Arnold, Schwinn & Company." They went into production immediately and began to market bicycles of the highest quality. America witnessed a bicycle boom: 25,000 bicycles left the Schwinn factory each year. Wherever competitions were held, Ignaz Schwinn was able to attract the best bike-racers in the country to his "Paramount Team." Schwinn was committed to combine in his bicycles quality, comfort, efficiency, and practicality.

Schwinn's business was booming, and technical innovations followed in quick succession. Around the turn of the century, Schwinn tried to manufacture automobiles, but he abandoned the project in 1905.

In 1903, Wilbur and Orville Wright, the pioneers of flight, used their knowledge of bicycle engineering when they designed their first flying machine. Nothing could stop the quest for faster transport.

The Reversal

Motorbikes, automobiles, and planes became so popular that they nearly killed off the bicycle, the same vehicle that presaged the existence of later vehicles. Manufacturing of bicycles declined drastically in the U.S.; the only demand was for children's bikes. But 90 years later, this trend was to be significantly reversed. Total motorization with its negative impact on the environment made the bike attractive again, and modern technology, knowledge, and the availability of new materials (like carbon fibre and titanium, once used only for planes and cars) made their way into the engineering and manufacture of bikes.

Ignaz Schwinn was the first to use the technology used in the automobile industry for bicycle engineering. His company survived the Depression and the decline in the demand for bicycles. To strengthen his company, he set up his own research department in 1930. His goal was to produce a bicycle that would feature a new design, be of high quality, and also be affordable. In 1933 he was able to introduce the

"Balloon-Tire Bicycle," which (a half-century later) was to become the mountain bike.

The Balloon-Tire Bicycle

In search of innovative bicycle engineering, Schwinn engineers learned about a new tire widely used in Europe, but still a novelty in America: a tire 1¼″ (3.2 cm) wide and equipped with an inner tube. They adopted this measurement, although it meant changing the entire tire-manufacturing machinery. Schwinn's engineers had another surprise: a new design similar to that of small motorcycles, a "streamline" design mirroring the trend then fashionable in the automobile industry. This, the "Streamline Aerocycle," was introduced in 1934, and it influenced the appearance of the American bicycle for two decades. From then on, the Schwinn company introduced a new model every year. Bicycle factories sprang up everywhere. Ignaz Schwinn had taken risks, and he had been proven right.

The Excelsior: Father of the Mountain Bike

Within a very short time the fanciful "Streamline Aerocycle" was upstaged by a scaled-down version, the "Excelsior," a comfortable, virtually indestructible one-gear bike with curved tubes, wide handlebars, and thick 2″ tires

The Schwinn Phantom, the most elegant version of the 1934 Excelsior. Spectacular novelties: wide balloon tires, extended wheelbase, and the first introduction of the trendy "Aero" design. The plainer version of the Excelsior became the favorite bicycle in America in the '40s and '50s, and is the father of today's mountain bike.

16

the bike of choice for most Americans.

New innovations from Europe suddenly appeared in the 1960s, first three- and then ten-speed bikes. These European innovations made the Excelsior seem rather portly. It soon fell into disfavor, and it was relegated to the dark corners of sheds or garages.

California—Land of Innovation

California has been considered the state with a great number of innovative ideas *and* the people to put these ideas into practice. It's a place where traditions are broken. For most people living on the West Coast, "freedom" and "mobility" are not just figures of speech— they've raised these concepts to a form of religion. For instance, in the early '70s, young people saw no reason why they could only ride their bikes on the streets; they burst out, off-road, with the result that bikes more suited to such riding were designed. What was "in" among motorcyclists was supposed to be just as much fun on the BMX, only here pow-

mounted on 26″ wheels, weighing 50 lbs (22.6 kg). To increase riding comfort and dependability, engineers combined wide, thick tires with a lower frame geometry. Soon the comfortable ride and superior handling of the Excelsior made it the darling of a new generation of youngsters, students, and commuters. Picture the

paperboy in old Hollywood movies . . .

Not only did Schwinn (virtually by himself) revive a slumping market with his keen business sense and innovative engineering, he kept it moving ahead by constantly adding new models. The result was a popularity of unprecedented proportions for bicycles like the Excelsior,

ered by muscle. Although the BMX fad disappeared almost as soon as it started, the motivation and direction bikers wanted to take remained.

"Clunker" Freaks

The late '60s was the high point of "hippy" culture in San Francisco. Gary Fisher, a bicycle racer (who moved his light show from one "happening" to another), and Charles Kelly (roadie of the rock group "Sons of Champlin") grew tired of the hectic life and traffic in the city. They moved from San Francisco north to Marin County in 1974. Like so many others, they were looking for a place where life was manageable and close to nature. It was in Marin that they met Joe Breeze and the "clunkers."

While others were busy tending their cannabis plantations, a few bike "freaks" got "high" from racing down the mountains at breakneck speed. The favorite downhill run, the one that gave those cycle "maniacs" the thrills they were looking for, was the fire trail of Mt. Tamalpais, near Fairfax. Gary Fisher worked as a part-time mechanic at a bicycle

A pickup truck transported the heavy "clunkers" and their riders to the summit; the subsequent downhill race was a thrill. Right: Joe Breeze; below: Fred Wolfe

shop in Fairfax and as a journalist for *Bicycle Magazine*. Charles Kelly also worked as a journalist. Kelly was the founder of the first mountain bike magazine, *Fat Tire Flyer*. These two were the leaders of a new biking movement.

"Repack" Races— Thrills and Test Drives

Racing bikes, because of the size of their wheels, weren't suited for "repack" racing—they just didn't hold up. While searching for a suitable alternative, bikers came across the old Schwinn "Excelsior" with its wide tires and 26″ wheels. These bikes could be had for a few dollars or just for the taking, and they were resurrected from their dusty garage corners. Because of the enormous weight of the "clunkers" or "balloon bombers" (as these Schwinn bikes were now called) and with only one gear, riding uphill was unthinkable. However, they could be quickly loaded onto an open pickup truck and driven up to the summit of Mt. Tamalpais. Now nothing stopped them from racing downhill at hellish speeds. They drove so fast that the grease in the coaster

brakes turned to liquid and ran out, making it necessary to "repack" the brakes, hence the name "repack race" for this adrenaline-producing downhill mania. Charles Kelly assumed the role of timekeeper and record keeper.

Mountain Bike Pioneers

All during 1976, Kelly and Fisher, together with Joe Breeze and Tom Ritchey, organized and steadily increased the number of repack races held at the 3-mile-long Cascade Fire Trail near Fairfax. Like-minded bikers from all around the area soon joined the fun. They met at irregular intervals; everyone knew each other, and they all had two things in common: They all wanted to own one of those modified "clunkers," and they all wanted to break the record for the 2.9-mile downhill repack race that covered a vertical drop of 1600 feet (500 m). They adopted the motto of the Hell's Angels: "Ride to live and live to ride."

There was only one problem: Even the sturdy Excelsior wasn't able to withstand the extreme punishment of these races. While Gary Fisher and Joe Breeze continued

to find new ways to improve the technology, it was Charles Kelly who saw to it that new races were scheduled on a consistent basis and that these California-style, two-wheel activities would become known beyond Marin County. The number of participants did indeed increase steadily. By 1979, the races became "happenings," with more than 100 participants and the presence of television cameras. Local authorities protested; it became impossible to comply with insurance requirements. The last race was held in 1984. Gary Fisher still holds the record of 4 minutes and 22 seconds.

First Changes in Engineering

Most of the "clunkers" had a 70° seat-tube angle and a 68° head-tube angle, with the upper tube ¾"–1¼" (2–3 cm) longer than was customary on racing bikes. They also had an elevated bottom bracket of 12" (30 cm), long chain stays of 18½" (47 cm), a long wheelbase of 45¼" (115 cm) and, of course, just one gear. Broken forks and damaged coaster-brake hubs were the worst problems. Forks and hubs were replaced with parts from girls' bikes, because girls were more careful riders. The next improvement was to use two-gear coaster-brake hubs manufactured by Bendix. Finding replacement parts and old Schwinn "Excelsior" frames became something of a sport among "clunker freaks." Much time was spent in old bike shops in search of precious parts. Old, but still usable, parts were like cash among "clunker freaks."

One of the first bikers: Fred Wolfe. His Schwinn "clunker" already has a double chain ring and a gearshift.

Stable Forks, Gears

Broken frames, forks, and handlebars, as well as the loss of grease in the brake system, became increasingly more serious during races and test trials. These problems stimulated efforts to find new solutions and improved engineering. Fragile handlebars and brake levers were replaced with forged-steel parts from motorcycles. Because Gary Fisher tired of having to be driven to the summit in a pickup truck, he was the first to install on his bike a five-speed gear system (in the form of a five-speed drum-brake hub), after an experiment with a three-speed system had failed. Charles Breeze wrote about this new gear system:

"In 1975, Gary Fisher found a rear drum brake on an old tandem bike. The heavy drum brake, made of steel, added even more weight to the bike, but Gary converted every one of his skeptical friends when, during their first outing, he left everybody behind on his five-speed clunker, despite the additional weight. Within a week drum-brake hubs became another sought-after item on the list of precious replacement parts. . . ."

Drum brakes in general became an "endangered species," just like 7¼" (185 mm) crankshafts with triple chain rings. These items were difficult to find even for racing bikes. "Clunker" owners were constantly on the lookout for these parts and they became creative do-it-yourselfers. By the mid-1970s, good replacement parts were very rare; needed parts just couldn't be purchased as they can be today.

Thumb Shifter, Handlebars, Quick-Release Mechanism

Gears arrived on the scene, and with them came the problem of where to mount the shifter. The headset was an impractical place, as was the frame. The rider's hands shouldn't leave the handlebars while riding over rough terrain at high speed; it's simply too dangerous. Again, it was Gary Fisher's brilliant idea to mount the gear shifter on the inside of the right handlebar. Now the rider could shift gears without getting into trouble. It wasn't the last time that necessity was "the mother of invention." Comfortably backward-curving handlebars were gradually replaced by more stable, less curved motorcycle handlebars; the result was much better off-road handling. The only other problem at the time was that the frame size remained the same. Schwinn "Excelsior" frames came in one size only; people come in different sizes. How was one to compensate for the differences? Gary Fisher to the rescue! He designed a quick-release mechanism for the saddle post; now it was possible to set the height of the saddle to match the length of the biker's inseam, giving the rider a lower (and much safer) position during rapid downhill rides.

Off-road biking was no longer restricted to downhill riding. A bike could go anywhere, on any terrain. Still needed was a special frame that had the geometry of the "Excelsior" but was much stronger. The wear during a repack race was excessive for the material used for the Excelsior's frame; and over time it became more and more difficult to find replacement parts.

The First Homemade Mountain Bikes

Almost every biker at the time owned an expensive, well-equipped racing bike. Everyone also wanted to have a highly specialized "clunker." In 1977, Charles Kelly asked his friend Joe Breeze, a professional frame builder from Mill Valley, to build him a custom frame. Breeze copied the geometrical dimensions of the 1937 Schwinn "Excelsior," using Columbus tubes. He added two stays on both sides, from the headset to the drop-out of the rear wheel, and from the handlebars to the drop-out of the front wheel (similar to the "knee-action fork," a fork-reinforcing device found on some of the expensive Schwinn models of the 1930s). These stays increased the frame's rigidity enormously, although the tubes Joe used were much lighter. Building such a frame was enormously time-intensive.

Sleeves that could accommodate the angles created by the new frame geometry weren't available, but *butt welding* would take care of those needs. Breeze added strong brake levers, installed the much lighter

Gary Fisher, then and now. He was and still is an innovative engineer and trendsetter.

cantilever brake system, steel handlebar stem and handlebars, and a five-speed gearing system.

Breeze (together with Otis Guy) was an exceptional tandem-race rider and was well known on the biking scene. He had successfully completed a frame-building course, and he was convinced that ten frames for the highly specialized "clunkers" would be plenty to "saturate" the market. Despite its weight of 37 lbs (17 kg), and its high price ($1500), the demand never ceased. Today the blue, glossy-painted "first mountain bike in history" is on display in a museum in Oakland, California. Charles Kelly's "Breezer," the second bike in this legendary series of ten, can be admired in the Mountain

Bike Hall of Fame in Crested Butte, Colorado. Joe Breeze also "parked" his Schwinn "Excelsior," the one that he used in repack races from 1974 to 1977, there.

The Bike Gets Lighter

Towards the end of the 1970s (by coincidence), the "clunker" movement profited from two trends that had developed on the West Coast. To increase the quality of the beach-cruiser (a single-speed bike with a rigid gear ratio, no brakes, elevated handlebars, designed for use on beaches only) as well as that of the BMX bike (meant for young people, 14 years old and up), 26"

aluminum rims were necessary. As was customary at the time, manufacturers in California bought some of their products in Japan at considerable savings. Wheel manufacturers, such as Araya and Ukai, promptly delivered. Cycle Pro supplied "Snake Belly" tires, measuring 26×2.125.

Other bothersome problems for the "clunker" crowd could now be checked off: heavy steel rims and traction-poor tires. The new rims and tires amounted to a savings of 6½ lbs (3 kg). In the meantime, triple chain rings made their appearance. Now it was possible to glide silently on a stable bike through narrow paths and across meadows and hills; one could escape the cities' oppressive traffic and enjoy nature. Even people who, until then, wanted nothing to do with bikes took a second look. A new sport was born, but nobody knew it at the time.

How the Mountain Bike Got Its Name

When Joe Breeze planned his trip across the United States, hoping to establish a new time record, he asked Tom Ritchey, a biking engineer *par excellence*, to build him a tandem frame for his mountain bike. Ritchey built three frames and sold one to Gary Fisher, whom he'd met at previous racing events. Fisher helped Ritchey promote this frame in Marin County, where the demand was still much greater than it was anywhere else. Overnight, the two started a company called "MountainBikes," the first official use of this name. An attempt to copyright the name failed because of its too-general character.

A Business Is Born

Tom Ritchey built the frames, Gary Fisher supplied the needed components, and Charles Kelly took care of marketing. These three weren't alone.

Don and Eric Koski manufactured the "Trailmaster," Jeff Lindsay the "Mountain Goat." Business moved along; the first four models (Ritchey's, Koski's, and two BMX-like "clunkers") were introduced to a skeptical audience at a trade exhibition in Long Beach in 1980. The craze at the time was the light, graceful racing bike. At first glance the mountain bike seemed to be slow and cumbersome. One year later, however, fifteen manufacturers produced their own versions of the mountain bike; the game of supply and demand had begun. . . .

Almost every model on the market looked like Ritchey's bike. Tom Ritchey's 1989 model, "Everest," had the following characteristics: tubes made from chrome-molybdenum-steel with $\frac{1}{20}''$ (1.2 mm) down-tube wall thickness, $\frac{1}{30}''$ (0.9 mm) for all other tubes ; sleeveless, with a 69° headset angle, Magura motorcycle brake levers on triangular "bull moose" handlebars; cantilever brakes from Mafac, with $6\frac{3}{4}''$ or $7\frac{1}{4}''$ (175 or 185 mm) crank arms; and triple chain rings from T.A. of France, the primary manufacturer of components; sealed "bull's-eye" hubs; and Suntour MP 1000 pedals with sealed ball bearings.

The "StumpJumper" made by Specialized, the first mass-produced mountain bike. Mike Sinyard saw the potential and his extensive advertising campaign made "mountain bike" a household word.

Worldwide Distribution

Yet mountain bikes were still very expensive; the average price was about $1200–1500, due mostly to the time-consuming process of building each bike individually and the difficulty of obtaining necessary components. Prices didn't change much until Joe Sinyard (from San Jose) came up with an idea. When he started his "Specialized Bicycle Imports," which carried a wide variety of bicycle components and accessories, he had a hunch that the potential for a real boom in bicycles and mountain bikes was inevitable. He bought four of the frames that Tom Ritchey had built and then had much less expensive copies made in Japan. He began to mass-produce the "Specialized Stump-Jumper" that differed from the original with a shorter top tube, a less fancy finish, and a cost 50% less than the expensive American-made version. He combined all of the above improvements with very aggressive marketing efforts, first in the U.S., and then in Europe.

Japanese Industrial Might

Additional momentum was created when Japanese bicycle-component manufacturers (through good business connections in California) began to watch with great interest what was happening. New companies, such as Shimano, Suntour, Sugino, Dia-Compe, and Araya were quick to react aggressively. They had already tried to compete in the racing-bike sector, but they'd run into stiff competition from Europe. All of their engineering efforts turned to research. The positive outcome of their efforts can be seen in every bike store: superior-functioning indexed-gearing systems, cantilever brakes, eight-chain rings, new handlebars and handlebar stems, sealed ball bearings, etc. Today Shimano and Suntour supply about 95% of all mountain bike components.

Bike Island

The worldwide increase in mountain bike manufacturing has taken on almost scary proportions. Having bicycles produced in Japan soon was no longer profitable. Taiwan became the "promised land."

Many frame- and parts-producing industries (particularly those producing handlebars and handlebar stems) sprang up practically overnight. Right now the island produces about 6 million bikes every year—50% of the world market. Huge companies such as Giant and Merida (the most popular companies) mass-produce and deliver complete bikes to the U.S., as well as to the European market. China and Korea have also joined in the game. Europe is also beginning to react, even if it is late. There's hardly one manufacturer of bicycles that doesn't have mountain bikes in its line; more and more models are being introduced.

Schwinn, Gary Fisher, Charlie Kelly, Tom Ritchey, and Joe Breeze are all involved in the mountain bike business. Many a "clunker" rider had some inkling of developments to come even if (in the beginning) they wanted nothing to do with a big-business boom.

The unbelievable popularity of the mountain bike is shown in the enormous increase in production, particularly as experienced by Taiwan. In later years the boom reached Europe.

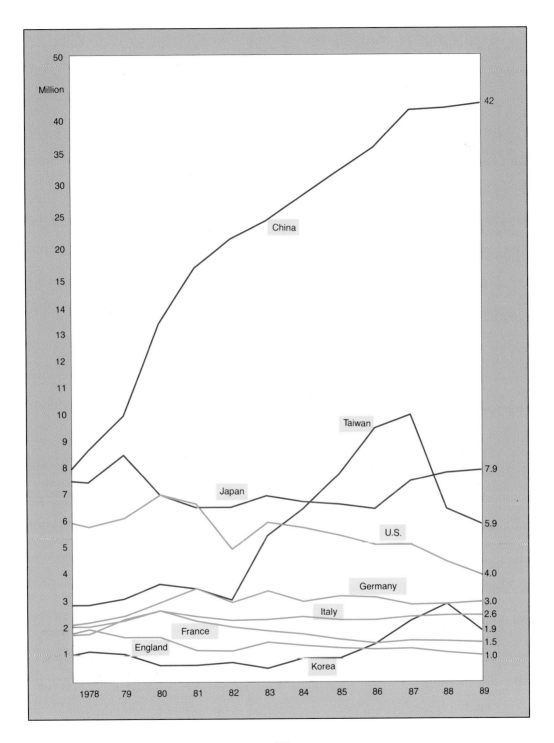

Different Mountain Bike Models

"MountainBikes," the name of Gary Fisher's and Tom Ritchey's company, was and still is the conceptual basis from which the whole mountain bike boom derives; the name "clunker" soon disappeared. With the increase of the mountain bike's popularity, however, the originally intended use was lost in many instances. Studies conducted in the U.S. in 1987 showed that approximately 70% of the mountain bikes never see off-road use—a sure sign that the mountain bike had become a status symbol. But it's also proof that this bike is exceptionally well suited to city traffic because of its size and its ease of handling. Reacting to the demand, many different versions of the mountain bike soon appeared on the market. A certain overlap within the following "subdivisions" couldn't be avoided. Today we distinguish among three types of mountain bike:

- Mountain bikes for sport (high-tech bikes, and racing bikes)
- Recreational bikes ("fun" bikes and all-terrain bikes)
- Utility bikes ("city" bikes)

What Makes a Bike a Mountain Bike

In the beginning, engineering and design leaned heavily towards concepts similar to those used for racing bikes. Together with the "clunker" experience, these trends resulted in the engineering of the first mountain bike. Despite these influences, the mountain bike shows clear differences from the racing bike.

A true mountain bike satisfies the following criteria:
- It is smaller in size than a racing bike, but it's longer, and it has a more rigid frame.
- It has a sleeveless tube with butt-welded joints.
- It has a solid, stable fork.

Mountain bikes can be roughly divided into three groups.

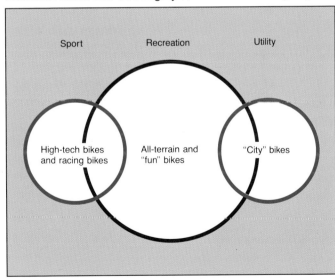

Sport   Recreation   Utility

High-tech bikes and racing bikes   All-terrain and "fun" bikes   "City" bikes

A typical racing bike for performance sport　　*The "fun" bike: comfortable yet sporty*

- It has wide tires with deep tread on a 26″ wheel.
- It has three chain rings.
- It has a large number of teeth on the sprockets.
- It has an easy-to-reach gearshift lever.
- It has rigid, almost straight handlebars.
- It has motorcycle-type brake levers.
- It has a quick-release seat post.
- It has cantilever brakes.

These were totally new concepts in 1980 and differed fundamentally both from the utility bike and from the racing bike.

These radical changes met with much skepticism among "traditional" bikers; the engineering was completely different from the light, elegant, aerodynamic racing machines. On the other hand, for those who wanted nothing to do with biking, this new concept expressed in engineering and components was cause for enormous enthusiasm. Innovation in almost all aspects separated this new machine from the "clunker"—a dynamic development that was, of course, not without its flops.

The Mountain Bike

The term "mountain bike" is not uniformly used. What follows is an (additional) attempt to establish a typology for this specific bike. The name "mountain bike" has many interpretations. "Mountain bike" might mean a high-tech bike, a racing bike, a recreational bike, an all-terrain bike, or even a "city" bike.

The High-Tech Bike

The distinguishing features of the high-tech bike include a very good frame made from the best materials available, eight freewheels, a gear lever (with an indexed system) mounted on top of the handlebars, an up-to-date frame design (for instance: specially mounted chain stays), oversize frame tubes, light tires, pedals without hooks, and light, solid, and perfectly functioning components. However, all of it is mass-produced.

The Racing Bike

The racing bike usually has an individually designed frame with a geometry that's typical for this bike. In addition, a

The all-terrain bike for every type of road surface   *The "city" bike: Ideal for town and country*

racing bike has very specific components, forks, springs, and tires. The tires always match different road conditions. Racing bikes are always the lightest bikes. Stability and susceptibility to breakdown are less important.

The "Fun" Bike

"Fun" bikes aren't build for any specific use. However, the frame and the components are of high quality. These bikes are also mass-produced and they're relatively inexpensive. "Fun" bikes have just the right combination of factors for those who've fallen prey to the mountain bike "bug" but who aren't necessarily interested in participating in competition. The difference between a high-tech bike and a "fun" bike is that although the latter also has

the latest components, these components are less "radical." A "fun" bike looks much like a racing bike, but its frame geometry is less severe and, therefore, more comfortable. CrMo-steel or aluminum is frequently used. Components, while similar to those of the racing bike, are less expensive. The "fun" bike is meant for enjoyment, even on long trips.

The All-Terrain Bike

For occasional off-road riding, the all-terrain bike is ideal. It has tires suitable for every terrain. It has the basic characteristics of a mountain bike. The more biking shifts from recreational to utility use, the more comfortable the frame geometry should be, and the more practical

the components, without sacrificing functionality. The bikes from Kettler are good examples; they were the first to use an aluminum frame.

The "City" Bike

These bikes, designed for use in cities, share many of the characteristics of the mountain bike, although in very reduced form. Sporty looks are subordinate to the needs of biking in city traffic. City-bike tires and gears are only marginally suitable for off-road riding. The "city" bike is about ¼ heavier than the mountain bike, due to accessories such as lights, luggage racks, fenders, and other heavy components. Nevertheless, many of the high-tech bike's components are used on a "city" bike as well.

Frame Technology

The frame, together with the fork, is the most important part of a mountain bike. Several important functions are combined here that, together, determine the use and capabilities of a mountain bike. A good frame must be light and strong, it must have maximum load-bearing capacity for riding over an extended period of time, and it must be able to withstand punishment and vibration. The best components are useless if the following needs haven't been taken into account:

Choice of tube
　Stability, weight, riding ability
Workmanship
　Safety, esthetics
Geometry
　Characteristics relevant to use
Design
　Functionality
Size
　Accommodates the human body

Pay special attention to the frame when buying a mountain bike. Choosing the right frame (considering the intended use and the buyer's budget) will bring the optimum benefits; the wrong frame will just bring problems.

Characteristics of a Mountain Bike Frame

There are four major frame tubes: seat tube, top tube, head tube, and down tube. In addition, there's the bottom bracket, tubing of the rear triangle, chain stays and seat stays, sleeves (seldom used on mountain bikes), the fork, and braze-ons. What makes a mountain bike frame different from that of a road bike? Many things, among others its history, the people who ride it, and its "philosophy."

The principles of today's road bike can be traced back to 1890 when, in England, the triangle frame was considered the best in bicycle engineering. The "diamond" frame was the best solution for a bike that was under stress from constant push, pull, and sway. Over the last hundred years, the diamond frame underwent slow but steady improvement and refinement. The wide angle of the seat tube became increasingly more acute, with the average now around 74°; the same happened with the head tube and the fork; the rear triangle became shorter. In general, frames for road bikes became smaller and more compact in order to increase rigidity and improve aerodynamics.

The mountain bike underwent a much more stormy evolution; within one decade, the design was radically changed. There are three reasons for this evolution. First, because geometry and design were copied from the first "Stone Age bikes"; second, because off-road riding posed different problems; and third, because innovative frame design mirrored the spirit of the times: young, new, oriented to problem-solving, dynamic, and strong.

While the evolution of the road bike took more than one century, the mountain bike evolved in one decade. The design of the old Schwinn "Excelsior" "clunker" was soon discarded due to experience gained with road bikes; hard off-road riding required extra stability.

Frame Geometry

It's important to know the basic frame geometry and how to measure it. The biker needs this information in order to judge the usefulness of a bike. The combination of tube length and angle determines not only the maneuverability of a bike, but it also determines the seating position and the transfer of power. What was, in the past, only of concern to frame builders and to serious race drivers is today the concern of hundreds of thousands of bike buyers. Mountain bikes are not all created equal. Variances of 1° of the headset angle, or 1″ (2 cm) difference in the distance between the rear-wheel axle and the center of the bottom bracket, can have very serious consequences. The basic elements of frame geometry are:

A Height of the seat tube
B Length of the top tube
C Seat-tube angle
D Headset-tube angle
E Trail
F Distance between the rear-wheel axle and the bottom bracket
G Distance between the front-wheel axle and the bottom bracket
H Wheelbase
I Height of the bottom bracket
J Stem angle
K Length of the headset tube

How do these values influence the maneuverability of a bike and how are they measured?

A. Height of the Seat Tube

The height of the seat tube is a basic measurement; it's determined by the length of the biker's inseam. For a mountain bike frame, this measurement is only of secondary importance because of the different frame designs and the different methods of construction used by different manufacturers.

Measure the distance between the bottom bracket and the point where the seat tube and the top tube are joined. In the case of a sloped top tube, measure as if the top tube were straight.

B. Length of the Top Tube

The length of the top tube should correspond to the length of the rider's trunk. With mountain bikes, unlike racing bikes, this measurement should be increased by a few inches (centimeters). This increases the distance between the axles, which guarantees more riding comfort and more stable and straight riding. Often the top tube slopes towards the seat tube, and for good reason: The bottom bracket of a mountain bike is about 1¼″ (3 cm) higher off the ground than it is on a road bike. In order to dismount easily off-road, the top tube is lowered.

Measure the distance between the points where the horizontal top tube joins the headstem at the front, and the seat tube towards the rear.

The geometry of a frame for a traditional bike. The top tube is parallel to the ground.

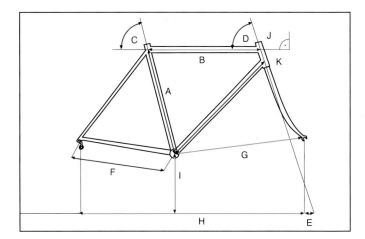

A frame with a sloping top tube. The height of the seat tube is the distance between the bottom bracket and the point where a straight top tube and the seat tube would meet if the top tube were straight.

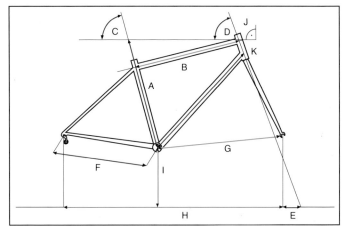

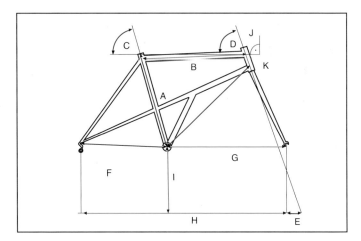

Geometry of a bike frame with a slightly sloping top tube, elevated chain stays, and a straight fork

33

C. Seat-Tube Angle

This angle primarily determines how a bike handles. While the angles at first were more blunt, today a 72° to 73° angle has become standard. A seat-tube angle of 69° to 71° gives a more comfortable ride; a sharper angle, however, increases a bike's agility and climbing ability. Riders with short thighs need a sharper seat-tube angle, while those with longer thighs need a blunter seat-tube angle.

Measure by holding a protractor against the seat tube, making sure that the bike is on a level surface.

D. Headset-Tube Angle

Together with the fork and trail, the headset-tube angle determines the steering characteristics of a bike. A steep angle together with a moderately curved fork reacts more sensitively when steering; a flatter angle reacts less sensitively. In the past, the headset-tube angle was approximately 68°; today, 71° has become standard.

Measure by holding a protractor against the headset tube, making sure that the bike is on a level surface.

E. Trail

The trail is the distance between two points marked by the extension of a line drawn from the center of the headset to the floor and by the extension of a line from the center of the front axle to the floor. See the drawings on page 33. The distance between the points depends upon the curvature of the fork and the angle of the headset tube. A longer trail makes for easy steering; a short trail causes the bike to react quickly to every movement of the handlebars.

Measure by extending one line through the center of the headset to the floor and by extending one plumb line from the center of the front axle to the floor. The distance between these points is the "trail."

F. Distance Between the Rear-Wheel Axle and the Bottom Bracket

The longer the span from the bottom bracket to the rear axle, the more comfortable the ride. A shorter span creates lively "action" and good climbing ability. The average span from the bottom bracket to the rear wheel for a mountain bike is 17" (43 cm); however, there's an increasing tendency to shorten this span. The span for racing bikes is between 15¼" and 16½" (39 and 42 cm).

Measure by taking the distance between the center of the axle at the rear-wheel hub and the center of the axle of the bottom bracket.

G. Distance Between the Front-Wheel Axle and the Bottom Bracket

This distance determines the amount of "toe clearance." Toe clearance means that the front tire and the tips of the biker's shoes never come in contact as the biker pedals and turns the front wheel at the same time.

Measure the distance between the center of the axle at the front-wheel hub and the center of the axle of the bottom bracket.

Measure the distance between the centers of both the front- and rear-wheel axles.

I. Height of the Bottom Bracket

This is the distance between the floor and the center of the axle of the bottom bracket. A lower bottom bracket makes the bike more maneuverable; an elevated bottom bracket means more stability and better straight-ahead riding, as well as a

quieter ride. A higher bottom bracket makes it easier to clear obstacles.

Measure by using a plumb line to mark the distance between the center of the bottom bracket and the ground.

H. Wheelbase

This is the distance between the centers of both the front- and rear-wheel axles. A long wheelbase means ease of handling and good straight-ahead riding. A short distance makes for sensitive, lively handling.

A perfect bike, a perfect body position, a perfect "pilot": MTB world champion Julie Furtado

J. Stem Angle

The stem angle is the degree of inclination of the headset tube. A wider angle gives an easy, comfortable ride, a narrower angle means a "sportier" feel. The comfortable angle is anywhere from 15° to 25°; for a sports bike the angle is between 0° to 10°.

Measure: Determine the total angle of the headset tube and deduct 90°.

K. Length of the Stem

A longer headset (stem) will distribute the weight of the driver more equally between the front and the rear wheels. However, it takes some time to get used to a longer headset tube. Longer headset tubes are more frequently found on racing bikes. A long headset tube is about 5⅛" to 6" (13 to 15 cm); a short tube measures anywhere from 4" to 4¾" (10 to 12 cm). Of course, these measurements shouldn't be considered separately. All measurements taken together, and their relationship to each other, define a bike's characteristics. The ability to interpret a frame's dimensions allows one to predict

Use	Frame Geometry
A. Comfortable riding	Shallow seat-tube angle—70/71° Shallow headset-tube angle—68/69° Longer distance between rear-wheel hub/bottom bracket axle—17¼" (44 cm) Trail—approximately 2¼" (6 cm)
B. Sports bike	Medium seat-tube angle—72/73° Medium headset-tube angle—70/71° Medium distance between rear-wheel hub/bottom bracket axle—17"/16½" (43/42 cm) Average trail—2" to 2¼" (5 to 6 cm)
C_1 For competition (ascending)	Steep seat-tube angle—74° Steep headset-tube angle—72° Short distance between rear-wheel hub/bottom bracket axle—15¾" (40 cm) Trail—approximately 2" (5 cm)
C_2 For competition (ascending and descending)	Steep seat-tube angle—73° Steep headset-tube angle—71° Short distance between rear-wheel hub/bottom bracket axle—16½" (42 cm) Trail for ease of steering—1½" to 2" (4 to 5 cm)
C_3 For competition (descending)	Medium seat-tube angle—72° Shallow headset-tube angle—69°/70° Longer distance between rear-wheel hub/bottom bracket axle—17" (43 cm) Trail: large—2¼" to 2¾" (6 to 7 cm)

a bike's maneuverability and allows the biker to determine if a bike will perform to his expectations.

Measure the distance between the center of the expander bolt at the center of the headset and the center of the handlebars.

Frame Geometry Determines Use

The dimensions/geometry of a frame determine the kind of riding the bike has been designed for. If a bike is used for leisure or weekend trips and it has the dimensions and angles of a racing bike, you've bought the wrong bike. If, on the other hand, you want to participate in

36

competitive hill-climbing events, a bike with shallow angles and long chain stays would be equally as disappointing.

The geometry of most mountain bikes is such that it will give the biker the widest possible latitude. The table on page 36 will guide and assist the consumer to buy the right bike.

The most important body measurement for choosing the optimum size frame is the straddle length, the distance between the crotch and the ground.

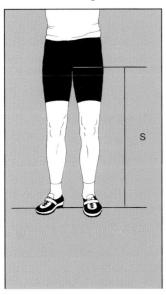

The variety of bikes on today's market is extensive; and finding the right one shouldn't be too difficult. If you're looking for a special mountain bike, it's best to have one made to order. Several frame manufacturers (except those that specialize in racing-bike frames) will build a bike to your own specifications.

Accommodating Frame Geometry to the Human Body

Once the primary use of the bike has been determined, a properly fitted frame to accommodate the biker's particular body measurements is very important. The machine should be adjusted to the biker, not the biker to the machine!

For a proper fit, the following measurements should be taken into account:
● Size of the bike frame
● Distance between the seat and the bottom bracket
● Distance between the tip of the seat and center of the handlebars
● Vertical difference between seat height and height of the handlebars
● Length of the crank arm
To calculate these measurements, first determine the biker's straddle height.

This is simple and uncomplicated: The straddle height is the distance between the top of the saddle (or the biker's crotch) and the ground (see the drawing on page 37). To measure, the biker stands erect and barefoot on the floor against a wall with a yardstick between his legs. The distance between where the top of the stick touches the crotch and the floor is the biker's "straddle height."

Knowing this measurement, anyone can easily calculate the proper frame size, as well as all the other measurements necessary for choosing proper frame size and the proper seating position.

Proper Frame Size

The proper frame size is calculated by multiplying "S" by 0.61.

This measurement, as shown in the drawing to the left is the distance between the center of the bottom bracket and the point where the top tube and the seat tube intersect. If the top tube is slanted, determine where the point would be if the top tube were straight.

$$S \times 0.61 = \text{Frame Size}$$

Suppose that "S" is 32" (82 cm). Multiply 32 by 0.61; this equals 19½"

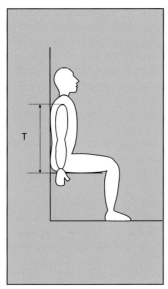

Calculating the length of the trunk (T). This value is also very important for determining the best sitting position.

(50.02 cm). The proper frame size would be 19½" (50 cm), meaning that the distance between the center of the bottom bracket and the (above-mentioned) point of intersection is 19½" (50 cm).

Only a few people will be able to afford a custom-made frame. Most must choose from the sizes that are available. Mountain bike frames are usually offered in three to five different sizes. The values given in the conversion table on this page almost always represent the distance between the center of the bottom bracket and the intersecting point between the hor-

izontal top tube and the vertical seat tube. These values are expressed in inches. The conversion chart shows the inch/cm values most frequently used.

Conversion Table

13"	= 33.0 cm
14"	= 35.6 cm (36)
15"	= 38.1 cm (38)
16"	= 40.6 cm (41)
17"	= 43.2 cm (43)
18"	= 45.7 cm (46)
19"	= 48.6 cm (49)
20"	= 50.8 cm (51)
21"	= 53.3 cm (53)
22"	= 55.9 cm (56)

The more choices a manufacturer offers for a particular model, the easier it will be to find the perfect frame size. The frames of most models come in 2" increments. What if the correct size falls between two sizes? Let's look again at our example:

We established a frame size of 19½" (50.02 cm), which falls between 19" and 20". Is the correct frame size the next smaller, or the next larger size? It all depends upon the length of the rider's trunk. Measure the rider (he should be seated) from the seat of the chair to the upper edge of the shoulder (see the drawing at the upper left). Generally, the trunk length is

about 75% of the straddle height. If the trunk is more than 75% of the straddle height, the choice would be the next larger size; if the trunk is less than 75%, choose the next smaller size.

The person in our example has a trunk length of 24½" (62 cm); that is 75.6% of the length of his straddle height. Therefore, in this case a 20" frame size would be the best. Generally it's better to choose the smaller frame. A smaller frame is more rigid, easier to control, and easier to steer than a bigger frame. These calculations come very close to the ideal frame size. Unfortunately, the misconception still prevails that the frame size is unimportant. Some say that adjustments can be made just by changing the height of the seat tube, and/or the headset tube. This is a basic mistake, since these adjustments are only "fine-tuning."

Ideal Sitting Position on a Mountain Bike

Proper sitting position determines the efficient transfer of muscle power to the drivetrain. To find the idea! position (meaning the proper height of the saddle) by trial and error can often take years.

Take solace, for even professionals need much time and often several frames until they achieve harmony between body and bike. But, it's easy to calculate the proper saddle height.

Several factors are important:
● Proper seat height
● Distance between the tip of the saddle and the handlebars
● Vertical difference between the top of the saddle and the handlebars

The basis for calculation (again) is the straddle height. By now we assume that the right frame size has already been chosen.

The proper seat height is calculated as follows:

$$S \times 0.885 = SH$$
$$\text{(Seat Height)}$$

"S" is multiplied by 0.885. Seat height is the distance between the bottom bracket and the top of the saddle. If the rider places his heel on one pedal that's been moved to its lowest point, his leg will be almost straight. Many won't be used to such a position, but muscles and tendons will adjust quickly.

For the person in our example, with an "S" measurement of 32¼" (82 cm),

the saddle height is calculated as: 32¼ × 0.885 = 28½" (72.57 cm) "SH."

The proper distance between the tip of the saddle and the handlebars is also very important:

$$S \times 0.66 = \text{Saddle-Handlebars}$$

"S" multiplied by 0.66 will give the proper distance between the tip of the saddle and the handlebars. Depending upon the length of the rider's trunk, the length of the

headset tube can now be adjusted in either direction. For the rider in our example this would mean: 32¼ × 0.66 = 21¼" (54.12 cm) Saddle-Handlebars.

The third important measurement, the height of the handlebars, also influences the transfer of power to the mountain bike's drivetrain. If the handlebars are too high, the leg muscles (for reasons of biomechanics) can't work efficiently; with the correct handlebar

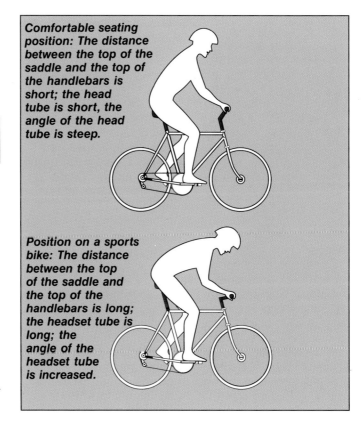

Comfortable seating position: The distance between the top of the saddle and the top of the handlebars is short; the head tube is short, the angle of the head tube is steep.

Position on a sports bike: The distance between the top of the saddle and the top of the handlebars is long; the headset tube is long; the angle of the headset tube is increased.

height, leg/muscle power can be used to its maximum effect—assuming the rest of the measurements have been calculated correctly.

The character of a bike can be significantly altered by changing the distance below the line defined by the top of the saddle and the top of the handlebars. A longer distance is appropriate for sports use because of good power transfer; a shorter distance is appropriate for recreational use, where the transfer of power isn't as important.

The desired distance can be calculated in two ways; first by adjusting the handlebar stem, and second by changing the angle of the headset tube. More about this in the chapter on the steering system. See page 65.

Length of the Crank Arm

Longer crank arms have become more acceptable. Crank arms on a mountain bike are 6¾" (175 mm) long, unless the bike is used primarily for recreation. Crank arms are even longer for racing bikes, 7" (176–180 mm). For less ambitious bikers a 6¾" (170 mm) crank arm is sufficient.

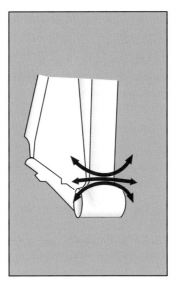

A bike frame is particularly susceptible to stress in the area of the bottom bracket.

The reason for a longer crank arm is obvious: Less energy is required from the biker. With appropriate conditioning, one can either drive faster or save energy; these are advantages for the racing driver but also useful for the recreational biker.

Maximum Load on a Frame

In order to understand why engineers choose certain raw materials, certain techniques for connecting tubes and components, and specific designs, one must know the stress to which a frame is exposed.

Engineers distinguish between a *static* load (the weight of the frame's material, the biker's weight, and the weight of his luggage), and a *dynamic* load (created through increased speed, uneven terrain, and braking). Both of these factors create pulling, pushing, bending, and twisting forces of considerable magnitude, and they're very specific for a mountain bike. See the drawing on this page.

The load from above comes from the biker, the bike's own weight, and possibly from any luggage that's carried along. A frame is very well suited to carrying this kind of load.

Side-to-side stress is created by an increase in speed, and when descending at high speed. The chain stays are under particular stress when the pedals are pushed with increased force. Lack of sufficient rigidity will cause considerable stress on the frame, especially when the biker pedals forcefully, increasing side-to-side motion; the bike may begin to "flutter" when descending. Stress from below comes from riding over obstacles. This *dynamic* stress is the most severe for a frame. Stress is more intense the greater the mass (weight of the biker and carry-on luggage) and the greater the speed. The lower frame tubes are particularly stressed.

Critical Stress to the Mountain Bike Frame

Critical stress will affect a frame at different points. The most severe stress is created from riding over rough terrain. Since such riding is "normal" for a mountain bike, the construction, choice of material, and technology used to connect the different parts are all of utmost importance.

In order to combat this enormous stress, the following criteria have been established for the construction of mountain bike frames:

Cross section of an aluminum oversize frame at the point where the top tube, lower tube, and head tube are joined. (Top)

X-ray of a welding joint in this area. This is a way to detect defects in the material. (Middle)

To strengthen this area of the frame, "Keith Bontrager" parts have been added, either by welding or by soldering. (Bottom)

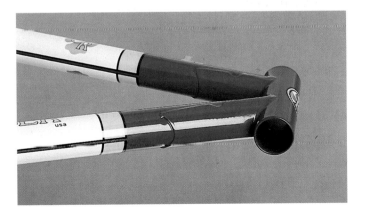

The beginning of an innovative development: Gary Fisher's "Excelsior" "clunker"

- A smaller frame triangle (the angles of a triangle remain stable even under the stresses of pulling and pushing forces)
- Elevated bottom brackets (increased rigidity in the bottom bracket, more room beneath the bottom bracket)
- Increased tube diameter (increased rigidity in the tubes)
- Increased diameter in the headset tube (better shock absorption and, therefore, better shock distribution)
- Oval, square, and rectangular tube ends (increases strength at critical points)
- Reinforced seat stays and chain stays
- Forged end points
- Suspension at the fork and at the rear portion of the bike (an advantage under extreme stress, such as downhill racing)

A tip: Take the exact measurements and check the workmanship when buying a new bike. Should an accident happen, measure again; possible deformation can be detected more easily.

Frame Design

Mountain bike frames have undergone many changes since the time when mountain bike pioneers used old, dusty Schwinn "Excelsior" frames. Joe Breeze was the first to design ten new frames that met the needs of the time. The enormous demands of off-road biking have, and still are, the driving forces behind innovative frame design. These demands were addressed by designers in California—Gary Klein, Richard Cunningham, Keith Bontrager—to name just a few. The design of mountain bike frames has undergone more radical change in 15 years than road bikes have in a century—and for two reasons. First, California designers (still the driving force in bike design) always search for something "new" and "better." Second, many of the designers are part of the still very strong in California BMX, and motorcycle scenes; many mountain bikers come from these environments.

Not only is high-quality steel used, but material from the aircraft industry—aluminum, titanium, and carbon-fibre—are common now. Today's mountain bike distinguishes itself by a sloping top tube, oversize tubes and headset, elevated chain stays, and suspension on both the front and the rear wheels.

With an increase in the bike's popularity, the bike's geometry has changed to conform to the motto

42

Above left: Classic and traditional. Diamond frame: The top tube is parallel to the floor. Right: Increasingly popular— aluminum frame with oversize tubes. The "Attitude" by Gary Klein

Below: The next step in design trends—a noticeably sloped top tube. The "Specialized M2." The "Kona" models by Joe Murray (below right)

Above left: The "net frame" is based on a design by Richard Cunningham, popularized by Bianchi. The GT All-Terrain Model (right) shows a reduced version. Right: Richard Cunningham's (1985) bike shows elevated chain stays for the first time.

Below: Unconventional designs—"Haro" by Bob Haro (note the curved top tube) and "Alpine Star" by Bill Stevenson (note the curved seat tube)

Above: Elevated chain stays lead to the next trend in design and technology: suspension—like the one shown on the "Off-Road" by Cannondale. Right: The "Sling Shot" has a flexible top tube and a down tube consisting only of a wire.

Below: Carbon-Monocoque-Engineering (C4 from the Italian manufacturers Bonfanti, Kestrel, and Trimble) and the Swiss aluminum body construction from S'Bike occupy a special position among the designers of mountain bikes.

"Steeper is better." The first mountain bikes had seat angles of 69° and headset angles of 68°; the combination 73°/71° is standard today.

The photos on the following pages give an overview of the frame's development and today's common frame construction. A mountain bike frame first must be extremely stable, functional, rigid, and, at the same time, flexible. Wide tires need sufficient clearance to remain free of mud; the frame must have good reinforced stress points, but it must, nevertheless, give the rider a pleasant riding experience. Tireless test riders and creative thinkers in California found a solution to every problem. They were praised for their innovative engineering, and for the visual excitement that they created.

Tube Material

More than 90% of all mountain bikes today are made from steel tubes. Of course, only high-quality steel alloys are used. Other substances that have been added guarantee problem-free manufacturing, as well as a high degree of stability, flexibility, and safety. However, even these exceptional steel tubes have one great disadvantage: their weight. Since weight is one of the basic problems of the mountain bike, there was ample reason to look for alternatives.

Aluminum has rapidly become the tube material of choice in the last few years. A decade ago aluminum was still an "exotic" metal, a label reserved today for titanium. The use of carbon-fibre and Kevlar has also increased. Since these materials had already been used in industries other than the aircraft industry, they've become more affordable. Today they are much in demand by frame builders because of their qualities: light weight, and good elasticity combined with strength. Carbon-fibre has been successfully used for tennis rackets, which themselves have had a stormy evolution: from wood, to steel, to aluminum, and now carbon-fibre. A similar progression is also anticipated for the mountain bike frame industry. Because the tube materials play such an important role in the way a bike reacts and feels, it's

Tube materials at a glance: titanium, carbon-fibre, aluminum and aluminum-oversize, and chrome-molybdenum steel. Each one of these will produce high-quality frames.

The Standard: Steel

For decades the frame-manufacturing industry had used chrome-molybdenum-steel in varying thicknesses to build frames for its better-quality bikes. A "good" steel assumes that a satisfactory compromise has been reached between the basic mechanical characteristics of steel and the effect of the changes soldering produces on the alloy combination. The two most superior alloys are 25-CrMo4 and 34-CrMo4 steel and they are used by such famous frame manufacturers as Tange/Japan, Columbus/Italy, Reynolds/Great Britain, Mannesmann-Oria/Germany-Italy, True Temper/U.S., and Ishiwata/Japan. In the U.S., this steel is known as "4130" steel.

The abbreviation 25-CrMo4 steel means that the steel contains 25% carbon (carbon makes steel tension-resistant, and serves as a protection against deformation); CrMo4 indicates how much of those substances that improve the quality of the steel (chrome and molybdenum) have been added. Manganese-molybdenum is also a very popular alloy. Both alloys reach very good antibreakage strength. Studies have shown that tension fractures of these materials decrease steadily at those portions of the tube that have been heat-treated. High-quality steel tubes have seamless joints, and their ends have been reinforced ("butted"). The strength of the walls of high-quality CrMo tubes has been tripled. Butted tubes are strongest at the point where two tubes are joined, and are weakest in the middle of the tube. Tom Ritchey and the Japanese tube manufacturer Tange together have produced outstanding, particularly light CrMo frame tubes for mountain bikes, because of the thin walls of the tubes and the way sleeves are used as connecting devices.

Advantages and Disadvantages of Steel Tubes

Producing high-quality steel tubes is relatively inexpensive, and they're ideal for frame manufacturing. Soldering produces strong, stable connections, even when automated processes (required for mass production) are used. Furthermore, steel is strong, and it tolerates a great deal of stress before it breaks down.

Steel's disadvantages are two: its weight and its susceptibility to corrosion. Frame manufacturers have been searching for alternatives that are lighter and don't rust. The fight against rust—even after expensive lacquers have been applied—is endless. Despite these shortcomings, steel-tube technology has made great strides, and steel remains the most reliable material for the frame industry.

The Alternative: Aluminum

Aluminum is the most frequently used material in the aircraft industry: it's lighter and softer than steel. This was known 100 years ago when the first aluminum bike frame was built. The pioneers in frame technology in Europe were Alan, Vitus, and Kettler. In order to make aluminum useful for mountain bike frames, an alloy had to be produced. Copper, magnesium, zinc, manganese, silicon, and titanium were each added; all of them increased the strength of the aluminum. The best-known aluminum

to the buyer's advantage to know something about the qualities and characteristics of these materials.

tubes are identified by 6061 T6 and 7075 T9 (by Easton/U.S.). The four-digit number identifies how much of other metals have been added; 7075 has twice as much silicon as 6061, and twenty times as much copper. T6 gives information about the thermal treatment of the alloy. In Europe, 7020 and 7075 aluminum have become the preferred alloys because of their high resistance to breakage.

However, maximum load capacity (the amount of pressure tolerated by a material before it becomes permanently distorted) of aluminum is not as high as that of CrMo steel. Strength, nevertheless, can be increased by widening the diameter of the walls of the aluminum tube—something U.S. frame manufacturers discovered in the 1980s. Gary Klein, Kettler, and Cannondale, among others, make frames from these "oversize" tubes.

Advantages and Disadvantages of Aluminum

The price for high-quality aluminum is as high as that for steel. However, depending upon the method used to connect the tubes, aluminum frames require more time to make. Either the tubes

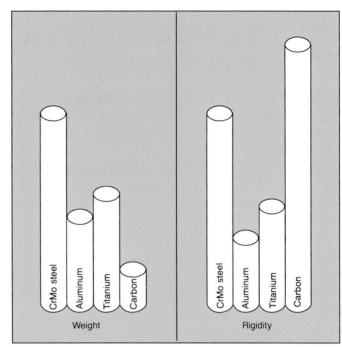

A comparison of weight (left) and rigidity (right) for the following materials: CrMo steel, aluminum, carbon, titanium.

are glued and screwed together with expensive sleeves, or they're welded together. Both methods are expensive and time-consuming. Done manually, they require skilled experts, or the use of welding machines. Although aluminum tubing has only one-third the rigidity of steel, when the diameter of aluminum tubes is doubled, the amount of rigidity is not simply twice but eight times higher. The remedy: oversize tubes which, for the above-mentioned reason, often have a diame-

ter of 2″ (50 mm). Another disadvantage of aluminum is its torsion strength. To improve torsion strength, the thickness of the walls of the tube has been increased; this, however, defeats aluminum's weight advantage.

There are three advantages of aluminum tubing for bike frames: Aluminum alloys are rust-free, they absorb shocks five times better than steel, and they're light. Because aluminum tubing can absorb shocks better than steel, the result is a more comfortable ride. For all of

49

these reasons, aluminum is used more and more frequently in the frame industry.

Titanium

This exotic material is most often used to make fighter planes. Because of its superior strength vs. its weight, the finished product is very light. In the past, this alloy turned brittle after time, resulting in small cracks under heavy loads. Nevertheless, with an adjustment in the combinations of metals that were used in the alloys, titanium is now stronger than steel. The problem with this frame material is its price and its complicated manufacturing process. In 1973, Europe introduced the first titanium frames for racing bikes; however, they disappeared rather quickly, due to cost-intensive production, early problems with the material, and lack of demand. In the meantime, alloy and production problems were solved, and, together with a new welding technique, the production of titanium frames has become much easier. In the U.S. today, mountain bike manufacturers (Merlin and Litespeed), and in Europe (Passoni/Italy), are successfully building frames with this material. These frames are seen more and more often in racing competition.

Advantages and Disadvantages of Titanium

The high price of titanium is still its greatest disadvantage; titanium is three to five times as expensive as CrMo steel. The welding method that weakens steel and aluminum has almost no effect on titanium; also, it's no longer necessary to do the welding in the vacuum chamber that was necessary in the past to protect the material against oxygen. A good titanium alloy (with vanadium and aluminum added) has approximately the same strength as steel, but it achieves only 60% of steel's rigidity. This problem is solved by increasing the diameter of the tube. High torsion strength is titanium's greatest advantage, a problem solved by making the wall of the tubing thicker. In addition, titanium is rust-free (the bronze-colored surface won't change after polishing and it doesn't need to be painted). Furthermore, titanium is 40% lighter than steel. If demand doesn't increase, an aura of snobbery will continue to surround a bike made with a titanium frame.

Tube construction: triple-butted CrMo tube (above) and a carbon tube with multidirectional fibre design.

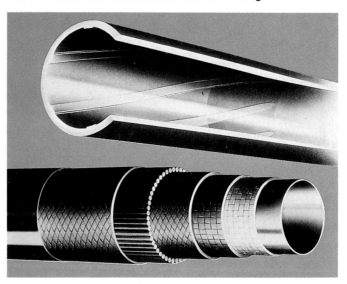

The Future: Carbon/Kevlar

Fibre and resin, a wonderful combination, is also part of the future of the mountain bike. The superiority of carbon tubes over steel, aluminum, and titanium is no longer a secret. This material provides great riding comfort, increased rigidity, and superior shock-absorption—precisely what is asked of a good mountain bike frame. Bike frames made of carbon are in great demand for racing bikes. These frames were also used for the first time in the Mountain Bike World Championship in 1990. Also, frames made from a combination of carbon-fibre and titanium are now being produced by Raleigh. Carbon has long been proven superior for road racing bikes: *Tour de France* winners of the last few years all used bikes with frames made from carbon-fibre. Two types of tube stand out: round tubes that are glued together with aluminum sleeves (Trek, Specialized, Yeti) and one-piece Monocoque frames (Kestrel, Ross, M4 Colnago). Besides carbon-fibre, tube manufacturers are also using glass fibre, graphite fibre, Kevlar, and Spectra. It's important in the manufacturing process that a correct, multidirectional arrangement of the fibres is employed to increase torsion stress. Inferior carbon-fibre tubes will fracture when exposed to heavy loads; they literally splinter. High-quality carbon frames give a unique riding experience.

Advantages and Disadvantages of Carbon

Although a carbon frame costs about four to five times more than a steel frame, it hardly has any disadvantages. Perhaps there is *one*: Monocoque frames have a very limited number of frame sizes (Kestrel has only two). But other than that, carbon tubes stand high above tubes made from other materials. Carbon frames are three times stronger than steel frames, and they have about 35% more rigidity. Today carbon tubes are well protected from corrosion, something that wasn't always the case. They once were very susceptible to "galvanic corrosion" (similar to what happens to batteries) whenever the aluminum sleeves used hadn't been sealed properly. Carbon tubes are 20% lighter than steel tubes; the sleeves used for joining the tubes add some weight, but in the end, carbon frames weigh 60% less than steel frames. Their excellent ability to absorb shocks (the energy flow of shocks is diffused by travelling from fibre to fibre) doesn't diminish the frame's rigidity. Carbon indeed is the ultimate material for frame tubes.

Frame Manufacturing and Technology

Today there are several methods available to connect frame tubing. For decades, bicycle frames were put together by inserting sleeves and soldering together the connecting points. Not until the mountain bike appeared were alternative methods applied. Sleeves made for racing bikes weren't useful because they couldn't accommodate the shallow angles of the mountain bike's geometry. Producing sleeves that would fit the angles would have been a costly undertaking, because the geometric dimensions changed so rapidly. The alternative was a sleeveless frame-connecting method, using *butt welding*. Today's gluing techniques make the use of sleeves possible again.

weakens the metal considerably. Much experience and concentration are necessary for this job. The advantage is that steel tubes are relatively easy to connect. The disadvantage is that oxygen can enter the seam and contaminate and weaken it. In the early 1980s, engineers in Japan worked on this problem and developed several new welding methods that are now used in Europe. Automation of the welding process is possible, and that's important for mass production.

Frame welding: Tubes and sleeves are connected with brass or silver solder.

TIG Method

The tungsten-inert-gas method is particularly popular for the manufacture of mountain bike frames. A high-temperature "light arc" melts anything with which it comes in contact. A tungsten electrode is used for such high temperatures. During the welding process, a ceramic tube continuously channels a gas towards the "light arc." This gas encloses the electrode, the soldering wire, and the connection to be welded, and, thereby, prevents contamination and doesn't allow oxygen to reach and weaken the area to be welded (this is very important when aluminum or titanium tubes are

The most exotic of all frame construction is the Monocoque form: A mold presses carbon plates (under pressure) into the desired form. Kestrel and M4 use this method for mountain bike frames. Let's look in detail at the different methods for connecting tubes for frames.

Welding

This popular and often-used method of frame construction is a process that can be automated, which makes it ideal for mass production. After the tubes have been accurately mitred, they're carefully heated to just below the melting point; a wire solder (with characteristics similar to those of the tubes) is applied to the seam. This is one of the most often used methods; however, it isn't without its pitfalls, because the tubes are heated almost to the melting point. Overheating

welded). What remains afterwards is a wavelike welding seam.

This method creates extremely stable tube connections.

However, this method also requires great skill, exceptional manual dexterity, and a steady hand. To make a perfect connection, the tungsten electrode should be approximately $\frac{1}{12}''$ (2 mm) away from the welding seam. Dangerous contamination that can weaken the tube joint would result if the electrode touched the welding seam. It's also important that the welding seam cover the whole tube wall.

Plasma Shielding-Gas Welding

This refined version of the TIG method eliminates the problem of contamination through the tungsten electrode. The tungsten needle retracts into a chamber, the "light arc" heats the inert gas inside a chamber and channels it through the ceramic tube to the seam to be welded. This method is particularly useful for connecting titanium tubes.

Impulse Shielding-Gas Welding

This method differs from the TIG method since the heat is regulated by means of an impulse switch. This allows for a more precise application of the solder; the result is an especially clean, wavelike welding seam.

Metal-Inert-Gas Welding

The difference between this and the TIG method is that a wire electrode is used instead of a tungsten electrode. This method allows the welding process to be automated. Many manufacturers use the method because they can make less expensive, mass-produced models with oversize tubes. These welding seams often show irregularities.

Soldering

Connecting frames with sleeves and brass or silver solder is widely practised, but seldom used for mountain bikes. The "mold-soldering" method, however, can be found more often.

Sleeve-Soldering Method

This is the most popular soldering method for road bikes. Because of the specific geometry of mountain bikes, the sleeve-soldering method is seldom used. After tubes have been cut and fitted, a sleeve is loosely inserted into both ends. After the whole area to be soldered has been carefully cleaned, it is covered with flux. Flux prevents the formation of oxygen (that would prevent the flow of solder) during the soldering process. The tubes are slowly heated to the melting temperature of the solder (usually brass or sometimes silver). The solder is held under the tip of the gas flame and allowed to flow between the sleeve and the tube. It is important to prevent overheating of the tube, because the result would dangerously weaken the material. Many metals are either difficult to solder, and some can't be soldered at all.

Fillet-Brazing

Tube connections made with the fillet-brazing method are esthetically the finest. Properly fitted tubes are covered with a rope of melted brass. The

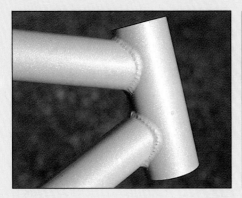

Above: Clean MIG welding joint, showing the dotlike welding seam.
Middle: Rope-soldering method— a rope of melted brass solder is layered over the seam.
Below: Glue connection. Often seen between aluminum sleeves and tubes, or

between aluminum sleeves and carbon tubes.
Above right: Aluminum-TIG welding. Wide, ropelike welding seams make the joint even stronger.
Below right: Sleeve-soldering— a clean connection is created between CrMo sleeve and brass solder.

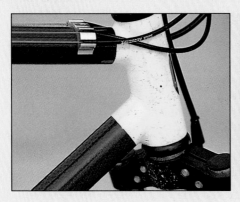

process of covering the seam with the melting brass solder is continued until a smooth surface covers the tube. Square connections are covered with an "overdose" of solder. Excess solder is later sanded down, and this can create a problem for the tube at the connection point. This soldering method, however, will accommodate any given geometrical dimension. It is, nevertheless, a time-intensive method and it's only found on expensive mountain bikes.

Glue Connections

Not until the middle of the 1970s was a suitable glue available for connecting tubes. Space research developed a hardened epoxy resin that turned out to be ideal for frame manufacture. The molecular structure of this resin is unique, because it can absorb and disperse loads that usually would lead to breakage. Tube connections made with this glue have a major advantage, since they aren't exposed to heat and they can't weaken the tube material. Sleeves, usually made from aluminum, are fitted to the tube, allowing for a small tolerance. Glue that hardens only when exposed to heat is applied to the ends at the inside of

the carbon-fibre, or aluminum, tubes and the connecting sleeve is forced onto the tubes. The frame is then heat-treated in an oven to cure the resin. Critical conditions that should be met during this process are: a specific temperature in the room, clean tube and sleeve surfaces, as well as correct tolerance between the tube ends and the sleeve. As additional insurance, some manufacturers don't just slide tubes into the sleeves after the resin application, but they screw them together. This method for gluing mountain bike frames is successfully used by Alan, Vitus, Trek, and Raleigh.

Connecting Carbon-Fibre Tubes

Most carbon-fibre frames are still produced by connecting tubes with the aid of sleeves; but producing these sleeves is very expensive. The future belongs to the one-piece frame. Several layers of carbon fibres are arranged in a "multi-directional" fashion with particular emphasis on the stress points of the frame that carry most of the load. After the fibre has been soaked in the resin, the layers are then forced into a mould with com-

pressed air. Seat tube, head tube, and bottom bracket are usually reinforced with aluminum. The advantage of fibre tubes is their strength; the disadvantages are a limited frame geometry and a limit in the number of sizes that can be produced. Each small change requires a whole new mould. This technology is being successfully used by Cycle Composites (Kestrel) in California.

Surface Treatment

The least number of rust problems occur with titanium, carbon-fibre, or aluminum bikes: All are virtually rustproof. The brownish bronze color of a titanium frame needs no paint. The same is true for carbon-fibre frames, which, however, are usually covered with a hardened clear varnish. Aluminum frames are not that simple to finish. The thin layer of lacquer covering the frame will prevent corrosion. But the paint may peel for two reasons: 1) tension corrosion (depending on the quality of aluminum) and 2) the layer of oxygen between the metal and the paint is capable of dissolving the resin. This can be prevented if the aluminum frame is put through a reduction process.

The Fork

The fork of a mountain bike commands much attention because it's exposed to a tremendous amount of punishment. Forks intended for road bikes will soon prove to be inadequate for mountain bikes. The process of improvement began immediately after the first fork became damaged during off-road riding. It wasn't long before the fork was *the* problem for the pioneers of the Repack races.

A fork design that already had a good track record among BMX enthusiasts was used for the first commercially produced mountain bikes. Some modifications have taken place over time (Oversize-Unicrown), but in general this type of fork is still standard for mountain bikes for two reasons: it's lightweight, and it's easy to manufacture. Engineers who'd switched from motorcycles to mountain bikes (like Keith Bontrager) developed a "straight," or "switchblade," fork in 1987. The jump from here to the spring-loaded fork was just a matter of time: "Rock Shox" became the first commercially produced suspension. Today one can choose among several different fork systems. Three types have different advantages and disadvantages.

Using the Unicrown as an example, let's look at the individual parts and the functions of a fork.

Fork Construction

The Unicrown fork has the following parts: fork-blade tube, fork crown, fork blade, fork-end drop-outs, and two bosses for mounting the cantilever brakes. Most of the time the "switchblade" fork has the same number of parts. The latter differs from the Unicrown in that the fork blades are exchangeable and they're straight (see the photo on page 59).

A well-functioning fork must have the following characteristics:
- Good steering ability
- Secure drop-outs
- Great stability
- Enough room for the fat tire
- Good shock absorption

The degree of curvature in the fork, together with the steering-tube angle, is responsible for the handling (steering) of the mountain bike. Assuming that the angle of the headset is constant at 70°, the following holds true: The larger the degree of bend in the fork, the greater the trail, and the more comfortable the handling. Less bend in the fork makes for a shorter trail, and an instant, "nervous" reaction to steering. If the fork blades are straight, the method of welding or soldering at the fork crown can simulate the effects of a bent fork. The drop-outs are important parts of the fork. Mostly made of steel, they differ by the presence or absence of a quick-release mechanism. If this mechanism is present, the drop-outs are not smooth, but have a round, slightly notched indentation at the outside; this prevents the wheel from falling out when the quick-release is used—a practical, precautionary measure that everyone who's lost a front wheel when landing after a jump will appreciate. Every mountain bike should be equipped with such a safety device.

The newest trend is the

use of extended drop-outs (GT All Terra). This means that the trail and, therefore, the bike's sensitivity to steering can be adjusted.

Suspension

Second in importance is how stable a bike is and how well it can absorb shocks. When hitting an obstacle, 80% of the shock is absorbed by the tire, rim, and spokes, and 10% by the fork; the remaining 10% travels to the frame and the handlebars. The 10% of the force absorbed by the fork is concentrated at the crown of the fork, or the fork blade. Most forks are flexible, and the blades bend (buckle) either forward (when landing after a jump) or backward (after a frontal impact). After a frontal impact, the down tube is also subject to buckling, usually near the headset.

These experiences with impacts had several consequences. The fork as well as the frame (down tube and headset) had to be strengthened in order to withstand the largest possible load. The diameter of the down tube and of the headset tube were increased (oversized) and, also, the diameter of the fork blade was considerably increased.

For "mud riders," it's also important that the fat tire have enough space between the fork blades as well as the lower headset crown.

Today many different varieties of forks are available: the standard Unicrown fork; the oversize Unicrown fork with straight, curved, or slightly curved blades; straight switchblade forks; and forks with suspension.

Unicrown Fork

This is the best fork for bikes intended for normal use. Its advantages are its low weight, approximately 17½ to 21 oz (500 to 600 g), as well as its good flexibility. However, this fork is not sufficient for racing bikes, which should have the oversize Unicrown. Increased diameter and wall thickness give much more stability, particularly for aluminum frame.

Oversizing, however, diminishes the fork's ability to flex. That's why so many oversize forks are either straight or have only slightly curved fork blades. Unicrown forks made from steel have a problem: The TIG welding or soldering method causes a steel tube to lose about 30% of its strength in the fork area. This can lead to

damage when the fork is subjected to an extreme load.

Switchblade Fork

Switchblades have straight fork blades that are screwed into the fork crown. The greatest advantage is that the steel tube is not weakened by welding. If the blades are damaged, exchange is easy. Switchblade forks have more stability, have a tighter feel, but they're heavier, 2¼ lbs (ca. 1000 g). In addition, it's even easier to manufacture a switchblade than a Unicrown. Despite all of its advantages, the switchblade fork is still rare.

Straight or curved forks? Curved forks are more flexible, straight forks are more rigid and stronger.

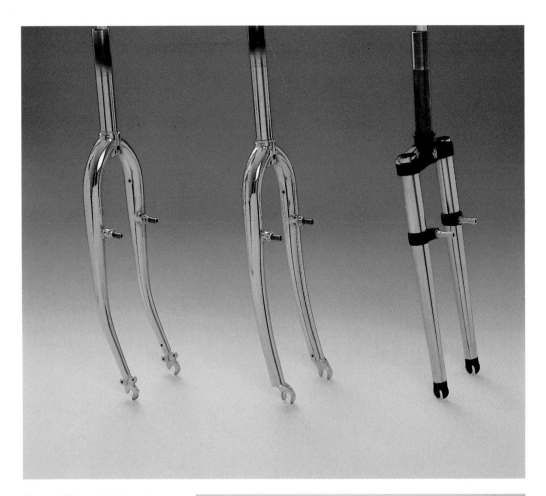

Three different forks: the standard Unicrown fork (left), the advanced oversize Unicrown (middle), and the switchblade, developed by Keith Bontrager (right)

Drop-out safety: The indentation at the edge prevents sudden wheel disconnection when the quick-release mechanism is activated.

59

Suspension Technology

Today's trend is towards mountain bikes equipped with suspension. However, it will still take some time until all the problems connected with suspension are solved. The demand for suspension is here.

The high demand for some kind of suspension system is because of the heavy load that the mountain bike's material must bear. Until now, the solution was always to increase the rigidity of the frame (oversize tubes, switchblade forks, strong rims, etc.). Strengthening the material compromised riding comfort. The logical consequence was to reduce strength by adding suspension to the wheels. Suspension technology was first used on bikes used for racing, since it was here that mountain bikes were exposed to the harshest conditions. In mountain bike races, 70% of the competitors use shock absorbers.

Front Forks with Shock Absorbers

The idea of suspension isn't new. It started in the U.S. with Paul Turner, who engineered the "Rock Shox." This suspension is similar to the suspension used for motocross forks.

This suspension consists of an aluminum fork crown with two telescoping blades that slide into each other when under pressure. The blades are made either from aluminum or steel. The distance of the spring action is about 2⅛" (5.5 cm). The degree of tension can be adjusted. There are two ways to absorb shocks: either with oil-pressure or air-pressure suspension (Rock Shox, Rock Soft, Star Fork, Scott, Fournales), or with springs and oil (Ceriani). Plastic parts (ATZ, Sticha) also give good results.

Advantages and Disadvantages of Forks with Suspension

Shock absorbers will react to pressure with a spring action of about 1¼" (3 cm) without damage to the different materials used. Front-wheel forks equipped with these shock absorbers don't lose contact with the ground, which allows for more control, and thereby makes driving at higher speeds possible. However, this advantage only comes into play when riding at high speed, and when shocks occur in quick succession. Suspension prevents shocks from reaching the tires, and thereby prevents damage to the rim; rims aren't as easily deformed, sprockets don't break as easily. The greatest disadvantage is the change in the ge-

Similar to the fork used on motorcycles, Rock Shox was the first suspension designed for the bike fork.

61

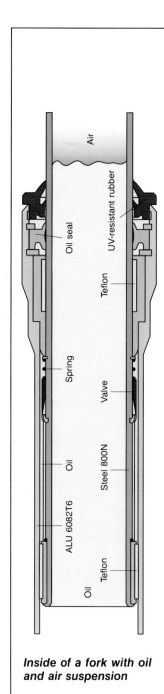

Inside of a fork with oil and air suspension

ometry of the bike: The steering-tube angle gets smaller, anywhere from 2° to 2.5°; the trail gets larger, which changes the handling of the mountain bike enormously, from characteristically quick to a sluggish steering reaction (something that's only advantageous in downhill riding). Add to this an increase in weight: A fork equipped with a suspension system weighs around 17½ oz to 2¼ lbs (500 to 1000 g) more than Unicrown or switchblade forks.

Suspension forks, because of their function and effectiveness, are particularly useful when the biker can't or doesn't want to avoid obstacles and when high-speed riding is the goal: in racing competition, and especially in downhill races.

For general use, suspension forks won't become useful until the system has been improved to:
● Minimize geometrical changes
● Design the suspension in such a way that it can be turned on or off as circumstances require
● Reduce weight

The same can be said for rear-wheel shock absorbers, but they have a whole different set of advantages and disadvantages.

Plastic elastomer provides the suspension of the rear wheel by Offroad (above), and that of Gary Fisher's RS-1 (next page).

The Sling Shot, with flexible top tube and down-tube suspension. Suspension action is distributed over the whole frame.

Rear-Wheel Suspension

After front-wheel suspension gained general acceptance, it was only a matter of time before the industry began to develop rear-wheel suspension, as well. An ambitious undertaking, because it meant jeopardizing the stability of the rear frame—a vital part of the frame structure. At the end of 1990, Cannondale, Offroad, and Gary Fisher introduced their first rear-wheel suspensions.

Cannondale and Offroad use similar systems: They both have elevated chain stays providing lateral sway, with the pivot point located in front of the seat tube. Seat stays are wishbone-shaped, meaning that the chain stays are above the tires and they end in a tube that's connected to the seat stay. It's here where the suspension is located. Cannondale uses an oil-pressure suspension, the Offroad rear frame is dampened against shocks by plastic devices. These solutions (in principle) function well technically, but they also contribute to some problems: Stiff wishbone construction at the rear frame lessens lateral stability; interference with the important geometry of the rear frame by adding shock absorbers will cause considerable loss to the bike's lateral stability, changing the ride of the bike.

Gary Fisher, the father of so many solutions to mountain bike problems, also makes a rear suspension device in his model line. The patent for it is from Mert Lawwill, who, using his experience from his motorcycle days, and together with Gary Fisher, installed plastic devices to absorb shocks. They're located behind the bottom bracket. Chain tension, however, makes the rear frame more rigid (due to lowered seat-stay position); traction is not affected.

Advantages and Disadvantages of Rear-Wheel Suspension

Rear-wheel suspension is great for riding downhill, because potholes are smoothed out, and tires are protected from severe punishment. However, uphill riding can be an energy-intensive ordeal when the rear of the frame bounces with every pedal stroke.

A bike equipped with rear-wheel suspension is also heavier. At this time no satisfactory solution has been found; the many different versions on the market are all still in the experimental stages. This technology is still in its infancy.

The Steering System

The steering system consists of the handlebars, the handlebar stem, and the headset. All three parts have seen a dynamic development over the last few years. High-tech materials and intelligent engineering have resulted in new designs and construction. It seems that the mountain bike attracts people who are always on the lookout for problems to solve and for new possibilities.

The steering system is one of the most important parts of the mountain bike, serving multiple functions. It not only steers a bike, but it also fills an important dampening and stabilizing function (10% of the shocks a bike receives travel from the road through the headset, the handlebar stem, and the handlebars). Last but not least, its design and position influence how much support the pedalling action receives. Even aerodynamic considerations have come into play lately.

John Tomac prefers racing-bike handlebars on his mountain bike because of the position that they give his body (he competes in road and bike races).

Handlebars themselves determine to a great extent the characteristics of a mountain bike. In the early '80s, the handlebars were still slightly curved towards the driver. Today they're only slightly angled, and on mountain bikes used for racing, they're almost completely straight.

Handlebars

All mountain bike handlebars have one thing in common with the frame: They're also made from steel, aluminum, titanium, or carbon-fibre. As for the frame, chrome-molybdenum-steel is still the favorite material for handlebars. In the beginning, a combination of a three-dimensional triangle design with a corresponding handlebar stem ("Bull moose") was popular because it increased stability. However, if somebody wanted handlebars or a stem with different angles or longer extensions, both parts had to be replaced, and this concept was soon abandoned. Mounting handlebars and stem separately makes it

easier to exchange or to choose between different combinations. Gary Klein's "Attitude," made from aluminum, is an exception. He combined the fork, headset, stem, and handlebars into an integral unit.

The diameter of most one-piece handlebar tubes is $7/8''$ (22 mm) at the handgrip, and at the places where the brake lever and the gear lever are mounted. At the center, where the handlebar tube is attached to the stem, most tubes are wider by about $1''$ (2.54 cm). This measurement is now standard. A handlebar tube is widened by forcing a separate piece of tubing into it. This piece remains inside and adds considerably to the overall strength of the handlebars. Handlebars without the widened center have an aluminum sleeve added instead, which corresponds in size to that of the bar stem. The wall thickness of the tube varies from $1/24''$ to $1/16''$ (1.0 to 1.6 mm) and depends upon the material used. In the beginning, mountain bike handlebars were $23 3/4''$ (60 cm) wide. Today, the average is $22''$

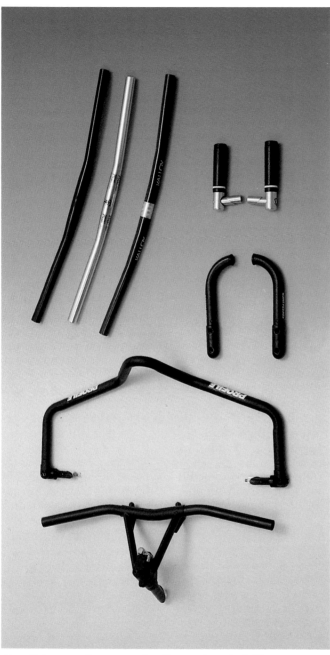

(56 cm). Racing-bike handlebars are even shorter, about 19¾″ (50 cm). The appropriate adjustment is very simply done by cutting the handlebars on both ends to the desired length. Handlebar tubes differ most of all in the materials used and in the specific characteristics they have. Everything that has been discussed in the chapter on frame tubing (see page 46) is also true for handlebar tubes. Aluminum handlebar tubing dampens shocks well; tubing made from titanium and carbon-fibre are even more efficient in this regard, but, of course, titanium tubing is also very expensive.

The trend in handlebar tubing, just as in frame tubing, is towards high-quality materials, because these materials are light and they absorb shocks well. The difference in weight is considerable: Handlebar tubes can weigh between 4 oz and 14 oz (120 and 400 g).

Another important design trend is the angle of the handlebars, which is anywhere between 0° and 12°, with an average of approximately 5° to 6°. There is, however, one exception: While all other manufacturers make handlebars that are angled towards the driver, the Odyssey Company, for ergonomic reasons, makes

Handlebars and accessories (from above): CrMo, aluminum, and carbon-fibre handlebars; inside- and outside-positioned "steering horns," an "aero-extension," and adjustable "bull moose" handlebars

66

Of particular advantage for climbing are "steering horns." Mike Kloser, shown at the 1990 World Championships, uses them extensively.

handlebars angled to the outside. The photo on page 66 shows the different shapes of three handlebars. Tubes are moulded by the cold-forging method.

The most important handlebar manufacturers are:

Steel: Sakae, ITM, Atax, Fisher, Odyssey, Salsa, Tioga
Aluminum: Answer, Syncros, Cook Brothers, Sakae, Profile, Fisher, Ritchey, Tioga
Titanium: Merlin, Fisher, Marin
Carbon-fibre: Profile, Polycycle, Nukeproof, Iko, Kalloy, Aerosport

Modified Handlebars

Normal handlebars have only one position for the hands. For recreational riding, this is sufficient, but sport and competitive cyclists have different needs. Horn-shaped handgrips, added to the handlebars at the time of purchase, are good for climbing; they give the rider a much stronger grip. Horn-shaped handgrips come in two different versions: They're either clamped onto the handlebars (Onza) or they're screwed *into* the handlebars (Syncros and Onza).

Some clever handlebar manufacturers, coming from the triathlon scene (like Scott and Profile), have taken this concept even further. Why should a mountain biker have only one hand position available? The handlebars with multiple handgrip positions were born and they were immediately successful. Scott uses a C-shaped tube made from 6063-T832 aluminum with a 7/8" (22 mm) diameter. An extension, made from a piece of plastic, attaches to both ends of the handlebars, creating a circle. One, the AT-4, comes in three widths: 20", 21½", and 23" (51 cm, 54.5 cm, and 58 cm), and weighs 12½ oz (355 g). The extension made by Profile can be attached to any handlebar (except those made of carbon-fibre). A connecting piece is wedged into the ends of each handlebar, with the extension attached to it by allen screws. The XC Durango is available in two widths: 20" and 22" (51 cm and 56 cm), and it weighs 13 oz (375 g).

Brake-lever and gearshift-lever mounting is a complicated procedure on handlebars from Scott, but it's not as complicated on those made by Profile, where the extension can be added or removed as the situation requires. In case of an accident, both versions have the same great advantage: The risk of injury is much reduced due to the blunted ends of the handlebars. The only disadvantage is that gearshift levers, like those from Campagnolo and Sachs, can't be mounted on these handlebars.

Four different hand positions are possible:
● Normal position for difficult terrain and for downhill
● Outside position when additional power is needed during climbing
● Hand position inside and parallel to the normal position for comfortable riding
● Gripping the "horns" for an aerodynamically favorable body position on good road surfaces

It takes some time to get used to different hand positions. "Horn"-shaped handles are not used very often, but it's nice to have the horns when they're needed.

Handlebar Grips

Handlebar grips play an important role: Wherever there is intense contact with the mountain bike (at the handlebars, saddle, and pedal) it's important to look for quality and good workmanship. Sadly, not all manufacturers see it that way. But what good are high-tech advances when hand and arm energy is wasted because

Ned Overend used an aero-handlebar extension for his winning ride in the 1990 World Championships. The closed extension made it possible for him to change to many different hand positions.

the grips are spongy, and might even slide around the handlebars?

Similar to BMX bikes, mountain bikes are equipped with strong but pliable handgrips, ¾" (20 mm) in diameter inside, and 1¼" to 1⅜" (30 to 35 mm) diameter on the outside. They're easy to install on almost all handlebars. They're usually made from a relatively dense but pliable material that's ergonomically fitted to the palm of the hand. Those grips made by Ritchey and Vetta-Gel are exceptional. A driver can hold on to them with full strength, and the ¼" to ⅓" (5 to 8 mm) thick layers of foam cushion the shocks that travel via the front wheel, fork, headset, and handlebars to the hands and arms. Under no circumstances should hand grips be moved after they're mounted; they must sit securely on the handlebars. Don't use soap or oil when putting them on.

Each grip, however, has its disadvantages: The plastic won't absorb perspiration, or the grips get slippery and the good grip is lost. Covering the grip with cloth, or with cork covers, is a good remedy. The best remedy, however, is to wear leather gloves.

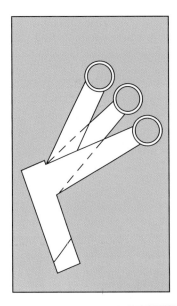

Characteristics of a handlebar stem: The steeper the angle, the "sportier" the bike; the flatter the angle, the more comfortable the bike.

Handlebar Stem

Aside from the fact that the stem supports the handlebars, it has a much more important role: The stem determines the best position for the rider's body.

Three measurements allow fine-tuning of the handlebar stem for the most appropriate body position: the length of the stem, the distance the stem can be raised above the head tube, and the stem's angle.

The length of the stem is determined by the measurements of the rider's upper body, arms, and the type of riding the bike is used for. The length varies between 3⅛″ and 6¼″ (8 and 16 cm). As a general rule, the more "sports" riding is done, the longer the stem. On mountain bikes, the distance the

Several different versions of handlebar stem construction (from left to right): steep-angled aluminum stem with a braze-on to hold the cable; aluminum racing stem with a braze-on for cables; extremely shallow and light CrMo racing stem by Tom Ritchey; CrMo stem with a power-support cable by Odyssey

stem extends above the head tube is kept to a minimum because of weight considerations. For recreational bikes, like "city" bikes, this distance is greater, to ensure a more comfortable ride. The angle of the stem also depends upon the use of the bike. The steeper the angle, the more "sporty" the bike.

Test this for yourself: The farther you lean over the handlebars, the more support your back gives to your leg muscles. See also the section "Accommodating Frame Geometry to the Human Body," on page 37.

Design of the Handlebar Stem

There are different types of handlebar stems: Most of them consist of one arm made from steel. "Recreational" mountain bikes often have a double-arm handlebar stem. The one-arm stem consists of three tubes, welded together: the clamping collar for the handlebars, the handlebar stem, and the handlebar extension that has a long allen screw and a wedge or cone-shaped device. Tubes often carry cables for the front-wheel brake. This

ensures good, effective operation of the front-wheel brake cable: Brake pressure can be applied in a more measured way. The disadvantage is that whenever changes are made to the handlebar stem, the brake-cable system is also affected. To circumvent this problem, a metal ring and a cable-guiding device can be placed in the headset.

Handlebar stems also come in a cold-forged, one-piece design. An allen-screw locking mechanism at the binder bolt secures the handlebar stem. A grey-iron wedge cone and a long, hex screw in the center securely join the handlebar-stem tube and the headset. The wedge cone ensures the greatest possible secure distribution of tension inside the tube without causing any damage. For sports bikes, a one-arm handlebar stem with a shallow angle is the norm. Oversize tubes made of high-quality chrome-molybdenum are particularly effective. A tube with a larger diameter and thin wall thickness has the advantage of weighing less. Handlebar stems made from aluminum don't have any weight advantages. To get the same resistance to distortion and the same degree of torsion strength, the

wall thickness of aluminum tubes would have to be increased considerably. High-quality steel is by far the better material. Titanium is the only other alternative for decreasing weight, but titanium is very expensive. However, the weight difference would be considerable.

Flexible Handlebar Stems

"Flexstem" is the name of the flexible stem used on Offroad's bikes. The man who invented it, Bob Gervin from Rhode Island, made the arm of a CrMo steel handlebar stem flexible by screwing a pivot at the tip of the stem. Exchangeable, elastic plastic rings in six different degrees of hardness serve as shock absorbers. Depending upon the weight, the length of the handlebar stem, and the needs of the biker, the plastic elements can be exchanged to accommodate any given situation. If a "hard" setting is chosen, the shock-absorbing effect (under normal road conditions) is not as noticeable; rough road conditions make one feel the difference. This shock-absorbing device was designed for the handlebar stem only, and it doesn't

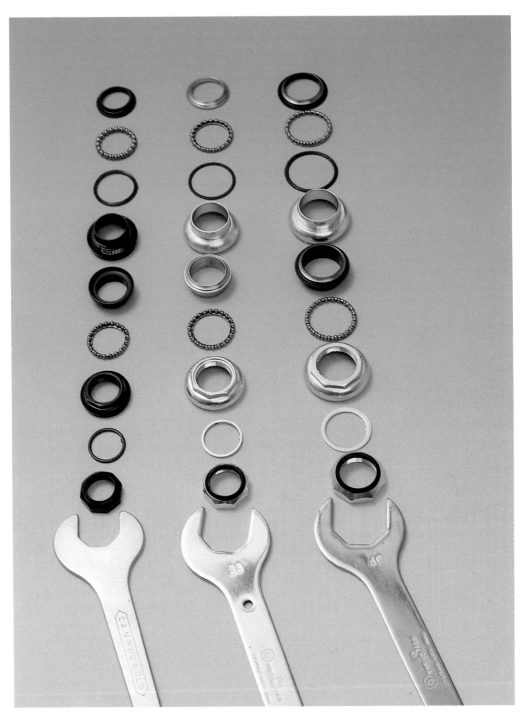

The three standard headset wrenches and their sizes: 1″, 1⅛″, 1¼″ (from left to right)

affect the rest of the mountain bike; however, it protects the biker from damage to his arms and shoulders.

Headset

The function of the headset is to allow for unobstructed free movement of the steering system. The headset also functions as a dampening device. It connects the fork to the frame, and it includes two ball-bearing joints. In the beginning, mountain bike builders had to make do with what was available. Joining the frame and the fork with a one-inch headset (originally designed for road bikes) was all that could be done. Soon it became apparent that a headset of this size was unable to withstand the extreme load created during serious mountain biking. The vertical and diagonal pressure on the axis of the headset is considerable. The lower ball bearings, in particular, are very susceptible to wear.

The ingenious inventor Gary Fisher went to work once again, and his idea to increase the dimensions of the headset (oversize) set the pace for the evolution and improvement in the design of mountain bikes. A larger headset tube meant larger fork-blade tubes and head-stem tubes; these changes affected not only the bike's steering performance, but the whole front end of the bike. An increase in the diameter of the tube made possible a decrease in the thickness of the walls of the tubing and, consequently, a decrease in the weight, while such an increase improved the rigidity of the frame. Fisher's "Evolution" steering system increased earlier diameter measurements by 1⅛", and later by 1¼", something that (at the time) caused a lively debate among the experts. By now, however, this concept has gained wide acceptance. According to Fisher, the oversize steering system has another advantage: improved road performance.

Components of the Headset

The headset consists of the upper and lower ball bearings, which allow the headset to rotate to the left and to the right. The fork crown is pressed onto the fork cone, followed by the ball bearings, the bottom headset race, and then the head tube. Headset races make mounting easier. The number and diameter of the ball bearings determine how well pressure is distributed. The upper portion of the headset consists of the top headset race, ball bearings, adjustable cup/top threaded race, the lock washer, and the locknut.

Perfect Adjustment

For a 1" headset tube, a double-sided crown wrench #32 is needed; for a 1⅛" tube, wrench #36 is needed; and for a 1¼" tube, wrench #40. A second wrench is needed as a counterforce. Adjustment is done by either tightening or loosening the collar or the locknut of the upper headset. The lock washer holds adjustments to the adjustable cup in place. The locknut must be tightened with sufficient force to prevent loosening of the steering mechanism. However, if this should happen during a trip, try to tighten it as much as possible by hand and look for the nearest repair shop. Most of the time, such an occurrence means having to replace the whole mechanism; because until the defect has been taken care of, the ball bearings will continue to suffer a great deal of damage. Since the addition of washers and locknuts, ball bearings are sealed to protect them from water, rust, and dirt.

Drivetrain

You still have to pedal all by yourself. How effective your pedalling will be depends upon how well power is transferred from the pedals to the crank arms, the bottom bracket, the chain rings, the chains, the rim, and the tires to the road. Much has changed since the first mountain bike came into being 15 years ago: pedals without hooks, chains that function well even under a full load, 8-sprocket freewheels with three chain rings, and all of these parts perfectly tuned to each other—all these technological advances that pioneers hadn't even dreamed of. All of these advances were made possible because of the boom in the bike industry, and the increase in research and development. Enormous demand engendered great

supply. As for many parts of the bike, the technology of the drivetrain also took a great leap forward; this technology has made the bike very interesting. What was once viewed and produced separately several years ago is now (since the appearance of the mountain bike) judged in its entirety. Chain rings, chains, and freewheels produced by different companies could not be matched and adjusted perfectly. It's to the credit of Japanese engineers to have recognized this shortcoming. Since compatible drivetrain components are now being produced, mountain biking has become so much more interesting.

Pedals, Pedal Hooks, and Straps

The pedals constitute another contact point between the biker and the bike. Here, muscle power meets machine. How that power is transferred through other components to make the rear wheel move is quite important.

Left: Constantly increasing in popularity—pedals without hooks, like those used by Julie Furtado

Right: A traditional pedal, consisting of pedal platform, hooks, and straps

Developed for specific use together with a corresponding shoe: the "Time" pedal and "SPD" pedal from Shimano

Interestingly enough, the mountain bike went through technological changes similar to those of the racing bike, and at a similar speed. But the results are much different; changes had to be specifically geared to mountain bike needs.

How independently mountain bike engineers have pursued their quest is best demonstrated by the pedals. In the beginning of the mountain bike boom, pedal design was greatly influenced by the BMX trend with its wide shoes. Specific shoes (like those for bike racing) didn't exist for mountain bikes. Pedals were made with "normal" shoes in mind. That was the thought behind the wide, bear-paw pedals, equipped with hooks.

These massive "universal" pedals soon became modified, improved, refined, and had less pronounced hooks. After all, a sports bike needed something better, and more elegant. The technology was there. After all, racing bikes already had their perfect, light, and elegant pedals. Mountain bike pedals only needed lighter hooks; the easily breakable metal hooks were replaced by wider, more resilient plastic ones. This modified pedal soon became the standard for mountain bikes, and, for a long time, this traditional pedal design was considered sufficient for the mountain bike.

But the unprecedented success of a hookless pedal system, introduced by Look, the ski-binding

company, in 1984, had found an ever-increasing acceptance in racing. Japanese engineers from Shimano began to experiment. They already owned 90% of the world's mountain bike business. They had noticed that a few mountain bike racers in the U.S. used hookless pedals for racing competition more or less successfully, since the system was designed for the road, and it soon proved to have its limits. When a mountain bike racer pushes down on the pedal, regular racing shoes turn into ice skates, and getting back on the pedals turns into a difficult task.

In 1987, the product manager of Shimano, Shinpei Okajima, began to work on hookless pedals for mountain bikes. Him-

76

self an active mountain bike racer, he and his team looked at the whole shoe and pedal problem. The end results: a hook-less pedal with double-sided devices to engage the shoes, and a shoe that still could be used for pushing all other pedals, as well as for running. They were called "Shimano Pedaling Dynamics" (SPD). The thick ⅓" (8 mm) soles were made with a cross-linking system of small plates. The advantage is to be able to quickly dismount off-road. In laboratory tests, the SPD shoe made dismounting possible in 0.46 seconds; for the old system 0.58 seconds were needed. Remounting proved to be even better: For the SPD system, 0.83 seconds, compared to 1.51 seconds for the old system.

The speed of mounting didn't decrease, even when the pedals were dirty. The SPD was also a technical improvement. The axle, made from CrMo steel was screwed into the body of the light-metal pedal. Adjustments are easily made with a simple adapter ring and a special key for the right inside ball bearing. A small disadvantage was the weight. The XT model with plastic hooks, plus the strap, weighs 13½ oz (380 g) for each pair. Two

SPD pedals weigh 17½ oz (500 g). Only the Shimano shoe can be used for the SPD pedal (at least until now). Other manufacturers, such as Look and Time, are pursuing the same idea. Both put plates into the soles of the shoes. The disadvantage of these models is that the bike can be mounted only from one side.

Bottom Bracket and Crank Arms

Almost all the bottom brackets on mountain bikes have the "BSA/BSC"

There's nothing like biking on nature's trails. Good, secure shoe-pedal connection plays an important part in the enjoyment of it.

system. In both England and Germany the standard size is 34.8 × 24 × 68 inches. The bottom bracket housing is threaded where the adjustable cups are screwed in, and where the ball bearings are inserted. Today, the greatest threats to the bottom bracket—dirt, moisture, and rust—have almost been eliminated, and not solely by using a sufficient amount of grease, but because most bottom brackets today have been completely sealed, as in those built by Mavic, Edco, and Kajita. These bottom brackets are virtually maintenance-free. Some of the larger manufacturers, such as Shimano, Campagnolo, and Suntour prefer open-bottom brackets that can be adjusted when necessary and that are protected from moisture and dirt by rubber rings and a plastic housing.

Examples of "open" (Campagnolo, bottom) and hermetically sealed (Sachs/SKF, top) bottom brackets

Crank arms are screwed to both ends of the four-sided axle, using a six-sided screw. In order to loosen this connection, a special device is necessary, which (after the six-sided screw has been removed) is attached to the dustcap. A fixing bolt screwed into the axle creates counterpressure, allowing the crank arm to be pulled from the axle.

Crank arms are made from lightweight metal alloys (Dural, for example); these alloys are an ideal compromise between light weight and high strength. The components are finished either by anodization or by polishing only. Cook's, of California, for instance, uses highly stress-resistant 7075 T-6 aluminum. As was mentioned on page 40, the length of the crank arm is also a very important factor. 6¾" (170 mm) is sufficient length for a "city" bike; for a sporty mountain bike, a minimum of

6⅞" (175 mm) is recommended. From road-racing competition we know that a longer arm requires less energy. For very demanding competition, like mountain racing or time trials, road-racing professionals use crank arms that are between 7" and 7⅛" (177.5 and 180 mm) long.

Once a smooth, "rounded" pedalling movement has become second nature, longer crank arms (given the same transmission ratio) require less energy. Mountain bike engineers have made use of

79

this knowledge and in-
stalled longer crank arms
on their bikes. Cook's offers bikes with a crank
arm length of 6½"–6⅝"
(165–167 mm) for children,
6¾", 7", 7⅛" (171, 176,
and 181 mm) for adults.
The real giants in the
industry have restricted
themselves to crank arms
between 6¾" and 6⅞"
(170 and 175 mm). The
exceptions are Suntour
and Tom Ritchey; they
also offer crank arms of
7" and 7⅛" (177.5 and
180 mm) length.

*Four chain rings from four
different manufacturers:
Shimano, Suntour,
Campagnolo, Sachs. Crank-
arm length is usually 6⅞"
(174 mm); chain rings are
again round and show a
tendency towards fewer
teeth (46/36/24). Sometimes
one can find an even lower
ratio, like "Micro Drive"
from Suntour (42/36/20)
and the "Compact Drive"
from Campagnolo.*

Chain Rings

Mountain bike technology
made a giant leap when
it began to consider the
most important parts of
the drivetrain (the chain
ring, chains, and sprock-
ets) as one system. Be-
fore that, each of the three
parts came from different
manufacturers. It's no
wonder that shifting gears
only functioned under
ideal conditions. Because
the mountain bike has to
withstand enormous loads,
limitations began to make
themselves known very
quickly.

Mountain bikers put up with the limitations inherent in the old systems until smart engineers from Shimano began to view the three-part system as a unit, and then conducted their research and development accordingly. The profile of the chain rings was changed, the chain-receiving points were determined through computer-generated measurements, the width of the chain was reduced and, as the crowning achievement, the sprockets were designed in such a way that even under enormous stress the chain would move "happily" from one sprocket to the next. Each part was improved upon, not in isolation, but in view of its effect on the whole system. Suntour did its development and research with the same concept in mind. Inspired by enormous competition, engineers in Europe began to think along the same lines. Campagnolo has already achieved the necessary engineering standards for mountain bike design; Sachs will reach that point in the near future.

Function of the Chain Ring

The chain ring fulfills an important function: the smooth and precise shifting of gears. On mountain bikes, the three different-size chain rings are mounted on the right crank arm. The two most popular chain-ring combinations are 48/38/28, or 46/36/26. The ten-speed system allows for a wide range of transmission, and shifting (the process of moving the chain through the gears) functions perfectly. The most favorable

Oval chain rings are "out," round are "in."

file of the teeth, the inside profile has an entirely different shape.

Round or Oval?

When analyzing the pedalling process, it becomes obvious that the amount and direction of power generated both change depending upon the pedal position. During pedalling, two "dead points" (where pedal movement is subject to different speeds) have to be overcome. This led to the following consideration: Would oval-shaped chain rings reduce loss in speed? The Puch Company was the first to undertake research. Shimano, after intense study under the guidance of engineer Shinpei Okajima, began to mass-produce oval chain rings. Shimano argued that a more natural and effective pedal movement was the logical result.

The argument itself has its validity as long as the number of revolutions of the crank arms remains low, 60 rpm. The secret of fast and efficient biking, however, is the ability of the biker to achieve high rpm. Only if a biker is able to combine a low gear with high rpm while biking can he hope to accomplish biking in high gear with high rpm, and only

chain movement depends upon the profile of the teeth on the chain ring.

Shimano (with the help of the computer) has located the point on the chain ring where the teeth create the least amount of pressure. In addition, the points where the chain is taken up and released are considered in relation to the teeth of the sprockets to each other. Gear-shifting—even when un-

der load—will function reliably. Suntour has also achieved this by a special mill-cutting method of the teeth which prevents the chain from falling between the ring or sprocket.

Wear on the teeth is obvious when they begin to look like "shark fins." In the past, one could simply turn the chain ring around. This technique is no longer possible. Compared to the outside pro-this makes high-speed riding possible. Since the rpm for sports biking, as well as for racing, lie between 90 and 120, the positive effect of the oval Biospace chain rings is lost. Not only is it lost, but it has proven to be a hindrance when compared to an efficient pedal movement achieved with round chain rings. The fact that more and more competitors in mountain bike racing seem to prefer round chain rings was not lost on Shimano's engineers. The extreme oval shape was reduced, and only slightly elliptical chain rings are still produced. Oval was "out," round is "in."

Whether round or oval chain rings are better depends most upon where the bike is ridden, as well as upon the preferences of the biker. Novices and those who only use a mountain bike sporadically will profit from oval Biospace chain rings. Trained mountain bikers, however, will prefer, for the reasons outlined above, round chain rings. Since much in technology is influenced by what's "in," oval chain rings have all but disappeared.

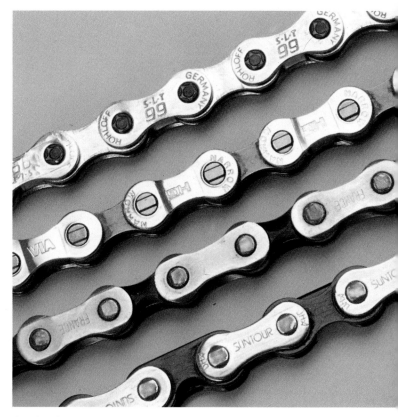

A selection of good chains. The most flexible is the top chain.

Chain

The chain plays an important role in a well-functioning drivetrain sys-

tem. Campagnolo, for instance, in its search for new designs for a totally different drivetrain system, designed the "Ritzel" chain ring. A good chain not only guarantees smooth gear-shifting, but it reduces wear and tear, as well.

A chain consists of about 60 chain links; a single link consists of two inside plates, two rollers, two pins, and two outer bushings.

Chain Functions

A new generation of chains evolved when Sedis introduced the first chain without bushings. An increase in side-to-side flexibility was achieved which not only improved chain movement, but also extended the life expectancy of the chain. Almost all chain manufacturers have now adopted Sedis' design. The manufacturer leading the field in producing flexible chains is

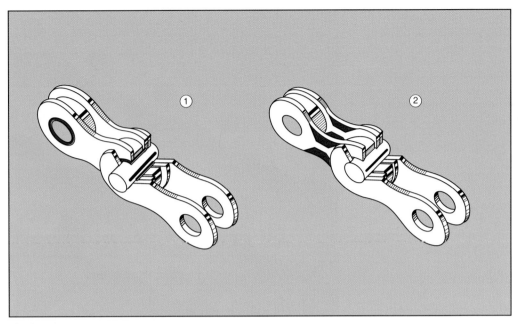

Older chains with bushings (1) were less flexible and wider. New chains, without bushings, offer more flexibility; they're narrower (2) and they're more "gear-friendly," due to plates that make chain movement easier.

Rohloff SLT: Its design has added even more flexibility. In addition, the company has shortened the outer plates, adding even more life to the chain. Campagnolo has adopted this design and all eight-sprocket bikes are equipped with these chains.

Of further importance for smooth chain movement are the inside and outside plates. Less side-to-side flexibility can be easily overcome with these components. Shimano and Suntour were able to affect flexibility positively by bending the outside plate, while Sedis did the same by bending the inside plate.

Another important factor is the width of the chain (8 mm-wide pins). In general, wide chains react more favorably to gear-shifting. By increasing the flexibility of the chain, it was possible to reduce its width; the average width, measuring chain pins, is $7/24''$ (7.3 mm). Rohloff chains are even narrower: $1/4''$ (6.85 mm).

Any chain will stretch under long and harsh driving conditions. The degree of stretch will influence the precision of the gear adjustments. After approximately 190 miles (300 km) of mountain biking, a definite stretch of $1/8''$ to $1/5''$ (3 to 5 mm) can be measured. The amount of stretch can be easily measured in the following manner: Place the chain on the largest chain ring, and then try to remove the chain. If the chain can be lifted more than $1/5''$ (5 mm), it must be replaced.

Freewheel

Within fifteen years, the number of sprockets on a freewheel has increased from five to eight. Today, the average is the five-sprocket arrangement.

However, Campagnolo already uses the eight-sprocket design in its production; Shimano and Suntour will introduce theirs in the near future.

Today the difference between freewheels is only in the design: The freewheel that screws in is being replaced more and more frequently with a "cassette" hub. For the "screw-in" type, the sprockets are screwed onto the thread of the rear hub; the "cassette" type has the freewheel mechanism attached into a notched profile of the rear hub and only the last sprocket is screwed on, locking the freewheel in place.

Right: Freewheels produced by Sachs, Shimano, and Campagnolo

Below: Teeth profiles from different manufacturers

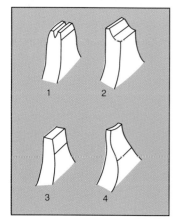

Cassette-Hub Freewheel

There are several advantages to the cassette-hub design: The first is the simple sprocket-mounting system; the second is the ease of exchanging sprockets, if that becomes necessary. Third, the rear wheel profits from the equal tension of the sprockets, reducing bothersome sprocket fractures.

Analogous to the relationship between chain rings and "teeth profile," the arrangement between the individual sprockets is also of importance. Campagnolo and Shimano have computer-generated measurements to arrive at an ideal arrangement.

Shimano's sprockets have slanted teeth on their "Hyperglide" system that correspond to the gliding angle of the chain. This, however, functions well only when a "Hyperglide" chain is also used. The engineers from Campagnolo achieve smooth gear-shifting by using three different "teeth profiles" that alternate and are brought into line with the next sprocket the chain is moving to. With the help of a table, and a specific combination of letters printed on the sprockets, the perfect profile combination can be found. If sprockets don't conform to this system,

the effectiveness is reduced by 20%.

Important for smooth functioning of the gears is the difference between the teeth of the sprockets that follow each other. The smaller the difference, the more efficient the shifting. Today's indexed gearing systems are designed for a six-teeth difference (for instance, from 26 to 32).

Gears

The mathematics are simple: seven sprockets in the back, three in the front = 21 gears. In reality, however, only 16 gears are available, for two reasons: First, extreme gears put undue stress on the chain. (With the largest chain ring in the front and the smallest sprocket in the rear, the chain has to accommodate an angle that's too wide, causing early wear and tear on the chain.) Try to avoid such extremes.

The second reason for the reduced number of "real" gears is that a bike will travel an identical distance with two different chain ring/sprocket combinations. For instance, the 48/24 combination gives you the same distance as the 38/19 combination, given the same number of

Jumping is only fun when the proper gears are used.

Conversion table for 26″ front wheels (distance in meters)

Number of teeth on chain ring

	24	26	28	30	32	34	36	38	39	40	41	42	43	44	45	46	47	48	49	50	51	52	53	
13	3.80	4.10	4.50	4.80	5.10	5.40	5.70	6.10	6.20	6.40	6.50	6.70	6.90	7.00	7.20	7.30	7.50	7.70	7.80	8.00	8.10	8.30	8.50	13
14	3.60	3.90	4.10	4.40	4.70	5.00	5.30	5.60	5.80	5.90	6.10	6.20	6.40	6.50	6.70	6.80	7.00	7.10	7.30	7.40	7.60	7.70	7.90	14
15	3.30	3.60	3.90	4.10	4.40	4.70	5.00	5.30	5.40	5.50	5.70	5.80	5.90	6.10	6.20	6.40	6.50	6.60	6.80	6.90	7.10	7.20	7.30	15
16	3.10	3.40	3.60	3.90	4.10	4.40	4.70	4.90	5.10	5.20	5.30	5.40	5.60	5.70	5.80	6.00	6.10	6.20	6.40	6.50	6.60	6.70	6.90	16
17	2.90	3.20	3.40	3.70	3.90	4.10	4.40	4.60	4.80	4.90	5.00	5.10	5.20	5.40	5.50	5.60	5.70	5.90	6.00	6.10	6.20	6.30	6.50	17
18	2.80	3.00	3.20	3.50	3.70	3.90	4.10	4.40	4.50	4.60	4.70	4.80	5.00	5.10	5.20	5.30	5.40	5.50	5.60	5.80	5.90	6.00	6.10	18
19	2.60	2.80	3.10	3.30	3.50	3.70	3.90	4.10	4.30	4.40	4.50	4.60	4.70	4.80	4.90	5.00	5.10	5.20	5.40	5.50	5.60	5.70	5.80	19
20	2.50	2.70	2.90	3.10	3.30	3.50	3.70	3.90	4.00	4.10	4.30	4.40	4.50	4.70	4.80	4.90	4.90	5.00	5.10	5.20	5.30	5.40	5.50	20
21	2.40	2.60	2.80	3.00	3.20	3.40	3.60	3.80	3.90	4.00	4.10	4.20	4.20	4.30	4.40	4.50	4.60	4.70	4.80	4.90	5.00	5.10	5.15	21
22	2.30	2.50	2.60	2.80	3.00	3.20	3.40	3.60	3.70	3.80	3.90	4.00	4.10	4.15	4.20	4.30	4.40	4.50	4.60	4.70	4.80	4.90	4.95	22
23	2.20	2.30	2.50	2.70	2.90	3.10	3.20	3.40	3.50	3.60	3.70	3.80	3.90	4.00	4.10	4.15	4.20	4.30	4.40	4.50	4.60	4.70	4.80	23
24	2.10	2.20	2.40	2.60	2.80	2.90	3.10	3.30	3.40	3.50	3.50	3.60	3.70	3.80	3.90	4.00	4.10	4.15	4.20	4.30	4.40	4.50	4.60	23
25	2.00	2.20	2.30	2.50	2.70	2.80	3.00	3.20	3.25	3.30	3.40	3.50	3.60	3.70	3.70	3.80	3.90	4.00	4.10	4.15	4.20	4.30	4.40	25
26	1.90	2.10	2.20	2.40	2.60	2.70	2.90	3.00	3.10	3.20	3.30	3.40	3.40	3.50	3.60	3.70	3.80	3.85	3.90	4.00	4.10	4.15	4.20	26
27	1.85	2.00	2.20	2.30	2.50	2.60	2.80	2.90	3.00	3.10	3.20	3.25	3.30	3.40	3.50	3.55	3.60	3.70	3.80	3.80	3.90	4.00	4.10	27
28	1.80	1.90	2.10	2.20	2.40	2.50	2.70	2.80	2.90	3.00	3.05	3.10	3.20	3.30	3.35	3.40	3.50	3.60	3.65	3.70	3.80	3.90	3.90	28
30	1.70	1.80	1.90	2.10	2.20	2.40	2.50	2.60	2.70	2.80	2.90	2.95	3.00	3.05	3.10	3.20	3.30	3.35	3.40	3.50	3.55	3.60	3.70	30
32	1.60	1.70	1.80	1.90	2.10	2.20	2.30	2.50	2.55	2.60	2.70	2.75	2.80	2.90	2.95	3.00	3.05	3.10	3.20	3.25	3.30	3.40	3.45	32
34	1.50	1.60	1.70	1.80	2.00	2.10	2.20	2.30	2.40	2.45	2.50	2.60	2.60	2.70	2.75	2.80	2.90	2.95	3.00	3.10	3.15	3.20	3.25	34
38	1.40	1.50	1.60	1.70	1.80	2.00	2.10	2.20	2.25	2.30	2.40	2.45	2.50	2.55	2.60	2.70	2.75	2.80	2.85	2.90	2.95	3.00	3.10	38
	24	26	28	30	32	34	36	38	39	40	41	42	43	44	45	46	47	48	49	50	51	52	53	

Number of teeth on sprocket

Conversion table for 26″ front wheels (distance in inches)

Number of teeth on chain ring

	24	26	28	30	32	34	36	38	39	40	41	42	43	44	45	46	47	48	49	50	51	52	53	
13	48	52	56	60	64	68	72	76	78	80	82	84	86	88	90	92	94	96	98	100	102	104	106	13
14	45	48	52	56	60	63	67	70	72	74	76	78	80	82	84	85	87	89	91	93	95	97	98	14
15	42	45	49	52	55	59	62	66	68	69	71	73	75	76	78	80	81	83	85	87	88	90	92	15
16	39	42	45	49	52	55	58	61	63	65	67	68	70	72	73	75	76	78	80	81	83	85	86	16
17	37	40	43	46	49	52	55	58	60	61	63	64	66	67	69	70	72	73	75	76	78	80	81	17
18	35	38	40	43	46	49	52	55	56	58	59	61	62	64	65	66	68	69	71	72	74	75	77	18
19	33	36	38	41	44	47	49	52	53	55	56	57	59	60	62	63	64	66	67	68	70	71	73	18
20	31	34	36	39	42	44	47	49	51	52	53	55	56	57	59	60	61	62	64	65	66	68	69	20
21	30	32	35	37	40	42	45	47	48	50	51	52	53	54	56	57	58	59	61	62	63	64	66	21
22	28	31	33	35	38	40	43	45	46	47	48	50	51	52	53	54	56	57	58	59	60	61	63	22
23	27	29	32	34	36	38	41	43	44	45	46	47	49	50	51	52	53	54	55	57	58	59	60	23
24	26	28	30	32	35	37	39	41	42	43	44	45	47	48	49	50	51	52	53	54	55	56	57	24
25	25	27	29	31	33	35	37	39	41	42	43	44	45	46	47	48	49	50	51	52	53	54	55	25
26	24	26	28	30	32	34	36	38	39	40	41	42	43	44	45	46	47	48	49	50	51	52	53	26
27	23	25	27	29	31	33	35	37	38	39	39	40	41	42	43	44	45	46	47	48	49	50	51	27
28	22	24	26	28	30	32	33	35	36	37	38	39	40	41	42	43	44	45	46	46	47	48	49	28
30	21	23	24	26	28	29	31	33	34	35	36	36	37	38	39	40	41	42	42	43	44	45	46	30
32	20	21	23	24	26	28	29	31	32	33	33	34	35	35	37	37	38	39	40	41	41	42	43	32
34	18	20	21	23	24	26	28	29	30	31	31	32	33	33	34	35	36	37	37	38	39	40	41	34
38	16	18	19	21	22	23	25	26	27	27	28	29	29	30	31	31	32	32	33	34	35	36	36	38
	24	26	28	30	32	34	36	38	39	40	41	42	43	44	45	46	47	48	49	50	51	52	53	

Number of teeth on sprocket

crank-arm revolutions. If the standard mountain bike gearing system for the chain ring is 46/36/26 and 12/14/16/18/21/24/28 sprockets, the forward movement achieved can be calculated using the conversion table on page 88. One will find that there are three overlapping gear combinations (46/18 with 36/14, 46/21 with 36/16, 36/24 with 26/18). If the two extreme combinations mentioned above are subtracted (small to small and large to large), only 16 "real" gears are left. Suntour prevents this situation to a great extent with its Micro Drive system (chain rings 42/32/20 and sprockets 11 to 23!). However, it's much easier to figure out the best gear combination by using the conversion table.

Inches are calculated by dividing the number of teeth on the chain rings, "CT", by the number of teeth on the sprockets, "ST", and multiplying the quotient (TT) by the diameter of the front wheel (in inches). For instance:

$$CT \div ST = TT \times 26$$
$$= 36 \div 12 = 3 \times 26 = 78.$$

The larger the gears, the greater distance travelled. Again, dividing the number of chain-ring teeth ("CT") by the number of teeth on the sprocket ("ST"), the result is "TT".

Then multiply the value π (3.1416) by the diameter of the front wheel (in inches) to get "F". Now multiply TT by F. Since the product of $\pi \times$ the front-wheel diameter (26) is constant, only

$$CT \div ST = TT$$
$$\pi \times 26 = F$$
$$TT \times F = distance$$

travelled per crank-arm revolution

Example:

$$36 \div 12 = 3$$
$$3.1416 \times 26 = 81.6816$$

or about 6.8 feet

$$3 \times 6.8 = 20.4 feet$$

In order to find the most favorable combination of gears, use the conversion table on page 88.

Gears

Something that we're almost unable to picture is that the first mountain bike had no gear shifter and only one gear. However, Gary Fisher soon changed all that; after all, he didn't just want to race downhill with his "clunker." After much time spent experimenting in the workshop, a gearshift system was finally mounted on his bike. But what about the gearshift lever? In the beginning (similar to touring bikes), the lever was mounted on the handlebar stem. But it was just too dangerous to take one hand off the handlebars in rough open terrain. That's when Fisher got the idea to mount the lever close to the hand grips. Later (but still during the early stages), the "freaks" added the triple chain ring, an idea that was also copied from the touring bike (T.A. and Stronglight).

Shifting and drivetrain technology have undergone enormous evolutions. Today it's possible to have on a mountain bike a combination of a quadruple chain ring and an eight-sprocket freewheel, provided the appropriate shifting system is installed. Gear-shifting is done by any of four different methods, and an "intelligent" index system allows for precise changes through the gears.

Gear-Shifting System

Today four different methods of shifting gears are available:
- Single-shift lever (available from every component manufacturer)
- Double-shift lever (Shimano, Suntour)
- Grip shifter, applied by turning the hand grip
- Ring shifter, installed in the hand grip
  Despite differences in application, all four systems have one thing in common: They're all indexed. The functions of the front and rear derailleurs have reached high standards, technologically and functionally. In combination with numerous gear positions this is (at this time) the most perfect gear-shifting system. The only disadvantage is that it needs frequent attention and adjustment.

Indexed Gearing System

To shift gears smoothly and silently before the invention of the indexed system was truly a difficult undertaking, at least for the beginner. It was a process of slow learning and only professionals knew how to do it properly. However, the indexed gearing system, invented by Shimano, made it possible even for the novice to master the art of shifting. The most important improvement was a built-in mechanism, where the lever engages with great precision, and where the derailleur moves in such a way that the chain rests securely on the chain ring, as well as on the sprockets. A simple concept that, nevertheless, requires a complicated mechanism.

The single, top-mounted shifter from Suntour

The double, underside-mounted shifter from Shimano

A somewhat different method of shifting: "Grip Shift" grip-turning shifter, from Sachs and Campagnolo

The invention of the indexed gearing system takes into account the changing geometrical situations within the system.

Perfect Chain Position

By providing a notched ring, the chain is always able to find the correct position on the sprocket and chain ring without falling in between, assuming, of course, the equipment has been perfectly adjusted. This perfection was possible because Shimano's engineers didn't look at the shifter in isolation, but as part of the whole drivetrain system. The result was a perfect union between gear-shifting and drivetrain, establishing a standard in functionality and developing a technology that was ready for its time. The considerable technological improvement by Shimano and Suntour is the reason why 90% of all mountain bikes are equipped with components from Osaka. While an indexed system is an advantage on road bikes (but not a necessary one) off-road, for all intents and purposes a bike can't be without it. Because a simple gear-shifting system would not only be less reliable, it would demand

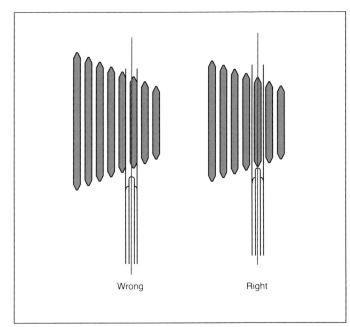

An important point for indexed shifting: Only when the chain and the sprockets are perfectly lined up will the drivetrain mechanism work perfectly.

too much attention from the biker. This is the reason why the indexed system is used almost exclusively by every manufacturer of components for all road bikes.

Shift levers are an important part of the gearshift system. Lately, levers used on motorbikes have also been used for mountain bikes. Gear shifters are the command center for the derailleur and the gears. The gears are moved with the right grip/lever, while the left grip/lever moves the derailleur. There are differences between individual levers and grips.

Single Shifter

As in the past, today the single shifter is the one most bikers prefer by far. In close proximity to the handgrip, and top-mounted, this one is the lightest—5¼ oz (150 g and up)—and reaches every sprocket within a turn of 90°. Single shifters also make it possible to disengage the indexed system, so that in case of difficulties, the gears and the derailleur can be manually employed, using the friction system. The only disadvantage is that the position of the lever isn't ergonomically perfect. The

thumb has to move up above the handlebars each time the gears have to be shifted. However, the single shifter system is still preferred for all racing bikes.

Double Shifter

For ergonomic reasons, a few bikers in the U.S., competing in mountain bike races, moved the shifter below the handlebars. With some qualifications, it functioned well if the biker pushed the lever *away* from himself. Pulling the lever *back* was the problem. Shimano and Suntour solved the problem when they introduced a double shifter in 1989. The lower lever moved the chain to a larger sprocket, the upper lever moved the chain to a smaller sprocket. The lower lever tightened the gear-cable mechanism, the upper lever used a step-by-step process to loosen the cable. However, the whole procedure became more complicated; instead of one movement in two directions, using one lever, now two movements, using two levers in two directions, was necessary. To shift gears it was necessary, even for trained bikers, to learn a whole new procedure.

Despite an improved ergonomic position, the

double-lever system has a disadvantage: Although by using the lower lever the largest sprocket or chain ring can be reached, to shift to a smaller sprocket (to the right), it's necessary to push the lever six or seven times (depending upon the number of sprockets), causing considerable slowdowns. Although this isn't important for recreational bikers, it is a concern for racers.

Grip-Turning Shifter

The great similarity between the mountain bike and motocross motorcycles can be seen in the similarity of their design and construction. The grip-turn shifter is one example, like the ones Campagnolo ("Bullet") and Sachs ("Power Grip") introduced at the end of 1990. The concept is the same: Handlebars with a diameter of 7/8" (22.2 and 22.7 mm) are equipped with a 6¼" (16 cm) long rotation grip with two or three spring mechanisms inside. These springs, activated by pressure, cause a mechanism either to tighten or to loosen the gear cable. In order to shift to another gear, the grip must be rotated. A dial (Campagnolo has its in a window, Sachs shows its by means of gradation)

lets the driver know on which sprocket the chain is engaged. Every sprocket can be reached within a 90° turn of the shifter.

Sachs added a lever inside the rotation grip that prevents the gears from jumping when riding over rough terrain. Campagnolo produced a "Bullet" grip with three springs, ideal for competition and improved shifting efficiency. Despite perfect ergonomics, both types have two disadvantages: The constantly increasing number of handlebar accessories leaves little room for mounting, and accidental shifting can't be totally eliminated.

Grip Shift

The "Grip Shift" is a system by Sram Corp. that can be mounted at several different places on the handlebars. A 2⅛" (5.5 cm) wide by 1¾" thick rotation ring can be mounted either on the inside or the outside of the grip and used on any handlebars that have 7/8" diameters (22.2 and 22.6 mm). An intricate, internal system consisting of three ring-cups that turn within each other tightens and loosens the gear cable by pulling it across a wedge. The only disadvantage is that a 270° turning radius is needed

to reach all the sprockets. The greatest advantage is its light weight. At only 2 oz (66 g) the "Grip Shift" is even lighter than the single shifter. In addition, other handlebar accessories can be easily added.

Front Derailleur

The front derailleur transports the chain across the three chain rings. This is accomplished by a chain guide (usually made from steel), which can be moved from side to side by a cable, and a parallelogram mechanism that's equipped with a retracting spring. Two adjusting screws at the front derailleur make sure that the inside as well as the outside movements are limited. When the first oversize tubes were introduced, problems arose due to the small diameter of the cage. Now, almost all manufacturers offer derailleurs with cages in various diameters that are fitted and mounted to the seat post of the mountain bike. Indexed systems also function with the derailleur, but still need further refinement. All too often the chain rubs against the cage and must be adjusted at the shifter. While this is relatively easy at the shifter, it's much more complicated with the rotation-grip shifter. Adjustments don't

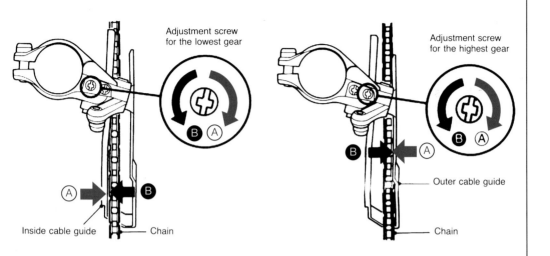

Adjustment screw
for the lowest gear

B A

Inside cable guide   Chain

Adjustment screw
for the highest gear

B A

Outer cable guide

Chain

Adjustments of the derailleur (a derailleur from Shimano is shown): Side-to-side movement of the derailleur is limited by two screws. After the shifter has been mounted, these two screws establish the basic position of the cage. The chain should not fall off on either side of the chain rings; however, the chain guide shouldn't come in contact with the chain, either.

To fine-tune the derailleur, an additional cable-housing screw is provided within the shifter. It serves to correct those small gear-shifting problems that develop over time due to stretching of the cable. Indexed systems demand trouble-free functioning and perfect adjustment and, therefore, constant attention and maintenance.

Cable-housing adjustment screw

B

A

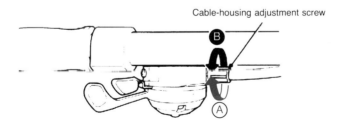

last, and frequent attention is necessary. This is a long-standing complaint about the rotation-grip shifter.

Rear Derailleur

The freewheel and the sprockets are much more complicated. In order to accommodate the wide arrangement of the gears, the mountain bike's chain housing has to be much longer than that for a road bike. In any case, the chain housing should accommodate the largest sprocket.

Since the patent for the "Slant" parallelogram mechanism has expired, almost all rear derailleurs are built according to this model. With the slant mechanism, a much better functioning shifting system has evolved (particularly for the mountain bike's enormous sprocket distances of 12 to 32), because the guide pulley "wanders" back and forth at the same distance— approximately $\frac{7}{8}''$ (2 cm)—over every sprocket.

Function of the Gear Shift

The correct distance of the chain between the center of the freewheel

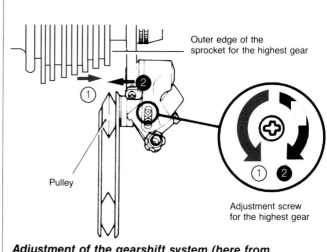

Outer edge of the sprocket for the highest gear

Pulley

Adjustment screw for the highest gear

Adjustment of the gearshift system (here from Shimano): The chain movement from the inside to the outside is established by two adjusting screws. After the cable has been installed, these two screws establish the exact basic position of the chain pulleys.

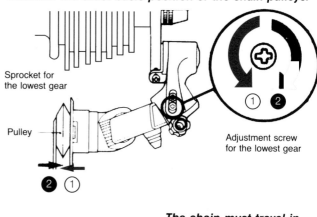

Sprocket for the lowest gear

Pulley

Adjustment screw for the lowest gear

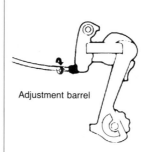

Adjustment barrel

The chain must travel in perfect alignment with the sprockets, trouble-free, and mustn't be allowed to fall beyond either the smallest or the largest sprocket. Fine-tuning can be accomplished via a cable-housing adjustment barrel situated at the end of the gearshift housing and inside the shifter.

Four de-
railleurs from
four different
manufacturers.
Note the dif-
ferent designs
of the chain
guides.

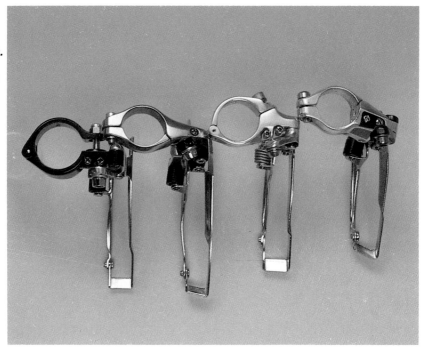

and the center of the up-
per chain pulley is important for a well-functioning
gear-shift system.

This distance should be
approximately 1½″ (4 cm).
If shorter, the guide pulley
would almost touch the
sprockets, and the chain
couldn't move freely
across them. If the dis-
tance is more than 2″
(5 cm), chain change
would be delayed. Good
pulleys are equipped with
ball bearings. Adjustment
of the gear-shift system is
accomplished by two ad-
justing screws (for inside

Gearing mechanisms are
almost all made according
to the slant-parallelogram
model.

and outside adjustments).
Exact positioning of the
chain is also possible
through an adjustment
barrel at the end of the

gear cable (at the gear-
shift housing) or at the beginning of the cable at the
handlebar shifter.

Brakes

Brakes are the only components that haven't significantly changed in the evolution of the mountain bike. Today (as in the past) the simple cantilever brake system has proven to be most reliable for off-road riding. Brakes still await their own revolution. Other brake systems, like U-brakes and roller-cam brakes, have been tested to replace cantilever brakes, but with little success. The continuing evolution of the cantilever system itself is significant, as seen in the Pedersen system. The future, however, belongs to disc brakes, which, at this time, are still in their infancy.

The concept of the disc brake is of interest for mountain bikes, because mountain biking makes such great demands on the brakes. These demands are best served by disc brakes for three reasons: First, the amount of space that disc brakes allow for the fat tires, so that mud accumulation won't create problems; second, the brakes should weigh as little as possible; and third, they must function under both wet and dry conditions.

Cantilever Brakes

The best system is a simple system, and one that works! The cantilever brake is a perfect example. Two movable brake arms with brake shoes (that can be pivoted in any direction) are mounted on bosses that are soldered to the seat stays, or to the chain stays. On many models (Shimano, Suntour/Dia Compe, Campagnolo) both brake arms are connected via cables. At the end of the brake cable, which originates at the brake lever on the handlebars, are cable carriers to which a linking wire is attached. Adjustments to the cable can be made either on the left or right brake arm, or at the cable carrier. The link cable can be disconnected either at the left or right brake carrier. This releases the tension and allows the rear or front wheel to be removed.

On newer models (Shimano) the brake cable, which comes from the brake lever, is attached directly to one of the brake arms, and, guided by a round cable carrier, connected to the other brake arm.

Typical cantilever brakes

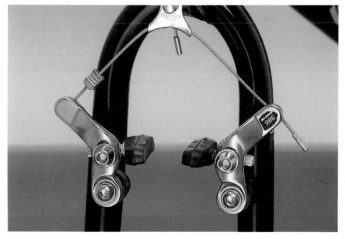

Cantilever Brakes and Their Improvements

On traditional cantilever brakes, the brake arms extend rather far to the outside for the best possible leverage. Sometimes this causes the rider's feet to come in contact with the brake arms. Grafton solved this problem with its "Low Profile" brakes. Brake arms became longer, but the angles became much tighter. In the meantime, both Shimano and Suntour have adopted this design.

The Pedersen cantilever brake (Suntour) makes use of the direction of the rim rotation to give more power to the brake shoes. The brake shoes are pulled in the direction of the wheel's forward movement, creating a correspondingly higher brake action. When releasing the brake shoes, a spring action pulls them back into the neutral position—an advantage resulting in an energy saving of 20%.

Brake Shoes

Most brake shoes are made from a hard, friction-resistant, special material consisting of vulcanized rubberlike plastic, which has been constantly improved over the years. New combinations made

Well-functioning brakes are of vital importance.

from synthetic rubber and phenol resin have increased deceleration, but overall they lose an enormous amount of effectiveness when the rims are wet—a big disadvantage with all rim brakes.

Since the rim becomes part of the brakes in cable-carrying systems, the effectiveness of the brakes is very much influenced by the surface condition of the rim. Mavic has recently introduced new rims. They've added a layer of ceramic to the outside of the rims (see also "Rims," on page 111), which has improved the effectiveness of the brakes under all weather conditions.

100

Other Cable-Brake Systems

Other brake systems having cable mechanisms somewhat similar in design to cantilever brakes such as U-brakes and roller-cam brakes haven't been able to stand up to cantilever brakes. Mountain bike manufacturers use them only sporadically, even if they are effective. They have long brake arms and an effective pressure-applying mechanism, and they do absorb rim vibration rather well. But their disadvantages outweigh their advantages: Both types are considerably heavier (approximately 7 oz [200 g] for each), and they're also very susceptible to dirt. Also, the mounting position behind the bottom bracket turned out to be rather cumbersome.

Hydraulic Brakes

Hydraulic brakes (like those from Magura) operate via an enclosed oil tube made from polyamide. Pressure applied to the brake lever is transferred to a cylinder and the brake shoes. In spite of many advantages (more effective braking with the same amount of hand action, variable cable-mounting options, and reduced loss of

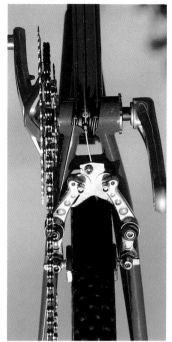

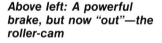

Above left: A powerful brake, but now "out"—the roller-cam

Above right: The U-brake is seldom used.

Right: The brake that sets the standard—the cantilever brake from Grafton

Below: Cannondale's improved cable system

power-transfer), these brakes are being used less and less, even though the last disadvantage has now been eliminated: In order to remove the wheels, one had to let the air out of the tires. The new model, introduced by Magura, solves the problem: Brake arms can be opened up so that the wheels can easily be removed without the inconvenience of letting the air out of the tires.

The Future: Hydraulic Brake Systems

Despite the cantilever brake's good record, the search for an effective disc-brake system for mountain bikes is in full swing. The Japanese bicycle giant Bridgestone is already experimenting with the idea. Mountain Cycles, a small, up-and-coming company in California, introduced a hydraulic "Pro Stop" disc-brake system at the World Championship competition in Durango in 1990. Aluminum discs (mounted at the hub through an interface) have brake shoes made specifically from low-temperature fibre material. These brake shoes grip the disc in a pinching fashion. The brake shoes, together with the aluminum disc, don't lose power or effectiveness even under wet conditions; braking efficiency is not diminished; power from hand pressure is perfectly transferred to the brake shoes. These disc brakes were developed in conjunction with a front-wheel suspension system (Suspender). Their weight, including fork: 5¾ lbs (2.6 kg). This system can

also be mounted on conventional Unicrown forks.

Brake Levers

The brake levers of the first mountain bike, modelled after those used for motorbikes, have been permanently improved in ergonomics, size, weight, and performance.

The lever pulls a brake cable, which transfers the pulling action of the brake arm of the cantilever (or U-brake) to the brake shoes. The lever was shortened after it was discovered that it can be operated with only two fingers. Since then two-finger, as well as four-finger, levers have been available.

Shimano increased the effectiveness of the brake lever by an ingenious roller mechanism. When the "Servo Wave" lever is

The roller mechanism of the SLR brake lever by Shimano creates a power-brake effect. The brake shoe is quickly pulled against the rim, followed by an effective transfer of power.

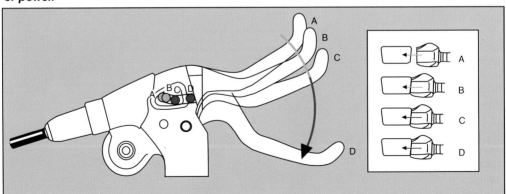

engaged, the pivot point changes in relation to the cable carrier—the closer the brake shoes get to the rim, the more effective the transfer of power from the lever to the brake shoes, all accomplished with a minimum amount of pressure applied to the brake lever at the handlebars. At the underside of the brake lever (under a rubber cover on Shimano models; left exposed on Suntour/ Dia Compe) are a screw, a nut, and a counternut, used to adjust the brake shoes. The closer the screw is turned towards the center of the handlebars, the tighter the brake cable will be, and the shorter the distance of the brake shoes to the rim. The biker can make adjustments without using tools. However, the initial adjustment should be made at the brake arms.

The Future: Hydraulic brakes that provide efficient brake action, in any weather—wet or dry

Right: The "Pro-Stop" brake, mounted together with the shock-dampening "Suspender" fork, introduced by the still-very-small manufacturer, "Mountain Cycles "

Wheel

Tires are among the most important components of the mountain bike, and they give it its own character. The term "fat tire" was the common name given to what we call today the "mountain bike."

The two main wheel characteristics are the diameter of the rim (26") and the width of the tires (1.6" to 2.5"). The tires usually have a deep tread. Smaller rims make a bike more maneuverable and more adaptable to trail conditions, where deep-tread tires are a necessity. In the beginning, steel rims and heavy tires made wheels very heavy. Now, however, aluminum rims are as thin as those used on road bikes, and the weight of the tires has also been drastically reduced.

As with all other bikes, the front wheel of a mountain bike is the one most subject to damage and defects. Tire defects, un-balanced rims, and broken spokes are the enemies of every biker. Maximum load has an enormous influence on wheels and the way they function. The "rolling" quality of a wheel is heavily influenced by the quality of its components (tire, rim, spokes, hub). In addition, both wheels form part of the brake system, and the rear wheel is part of the drivetrain.

Tires

Wide "wire" tires have characterized the mountain bike as no other component has. Wire is in quotes, because wire and linen fibre are seldom used anymore in tire manufacturing. They've been replaced by man-made fibres such as nylon and Kevlar. A typical mountain bike tire has the following characteristics:

● The body consists of several layers of fibre; a wire mesh or a flexible plastic (like Aramid) reinforces the edges, where the tire is mounted into the rim. This adds flexibility to the tire.

Wide, thick tires, and a deep tread: These are the characteristics of a mountain bike tire.

● The surface consists of a layer of rubber into which the tread is carved. The tread determines the traction and the rollability of the wheel. Some mountain bike tires (used for competition) are equipped with inner tubes. Such tires provide better protection against shocks, due to the small rim. Tires with inner tubes also provide better rollability, but there's no weight advantage. In addition, mounting is more complicated (the inner tube is glued with a special glue to a flatbed rim). "Wire" tires are more practical, easier to handle and, therefore, much preferred.

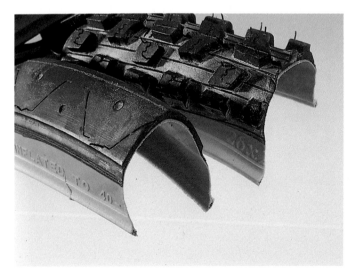

Above: Different dimensions, different treads. From right to left: Avocet City Slick 1.5; Avocet Cross 1.5; Ritchey Quad 1.6; Panaracer Khartoum 2.0; Specialized Extreme 2.5

Cross section of two tires. Clearly visible are: the depth of the tread, the layers making up the body, and the wire at the edges of the tires.

Tire Dimensions and Tread

Typical dimensions of U.S. bike tires (in inches) have also become the standard for all other bike tires. The dimensions are expressed by two values that are always printed (together with a number listing the required air pressure) on the outside wall of each tire: the diameter of the wheel and the width of the tire. The figures 26 × 1.95 mean that the diameter of the wheel is 26″ (66 cm) and that the tire is 1.95″ (4.95 cm) wide. Mountain bike tires are anywhere between 1″ and 2.5″, with the majority measuring 1.95″.

The next difference is in the type of tread. There are:

- Tires without tread
- Tread with a drainage channel
- Tires with blank centers and tread on the outside edges
- Tread that simulates drainage channels
- Pure, deep tread

The choice of a tread will depend upon the intended use of the tire and the air pressure necessary for it. The rougher the terrain, the deeper the

Something obviously went wrong. The tire and the rim react quickly when the "load" is too great.

109

tread and the greater the air pressure required.

Tire Functions

A tire has three functions:
- To provide "rollability"
- To provide traction
- To provide safe surface contact

Good "rollability" is influenced by a flexible tire body and the choice of the correct tread. Casings are provided with better flexibility by using a specific weaving method. The tread should accommodate the type of road surface the bike is intended to be used on most frequently. "Slicks" are good for asphalt and stone surfaces, because the soft rubber adheres particularly well to the road surface, even when the surface is wet. However, try to avoid riding on wet grass or leaves. Tires with drainage channels or tires that simulate drainage channels are good on asphalt as well as for off-road riding. These and the "all-purpose" tires, although they don't meet all needs, present a good compromise.

Off-road tires are available with different treads. Riding on asphalt, they often give an unbalanced feeling, and they're noisy. However, in sandy, earthy, and soft terrain, tires with deep tread are outstanding because of their supe-

rior traction. The tire also serves as an important dampening device: 80% of the enormous pressure coming from the road surface is absorbed by the wheel; the tire is "first in the line of fire." Most dreaded is the effect of impact shocks. If the impact exceeds a certain degree, the inner tube is compressed against the body of the tire, at the rim. The result is a damaged tire. Proper air pressure and the proper tire width are the best means of countering this.

Air Pressure

The appropriate air pressure is printed on the outside of the tire wall, and it's expressed in PSI (pressure per square inch); depending upon the type of tire, the range is between 35 and 65 PSI. This corresponds to an air-pressure value of 2.38 and 4.42 bar. (In order to calculate "bar," PSI is multiplied by 0.068). The amount of air pressure determines the shock-dampening ability of the tire. Low pressure increases the resistance to "rollability" and the danger of damage to the tires.

Weight

Tire weight varies between 18 and 36 oz (500 and 1000 g); the average

weight for most tires is about 23 to 26 oz (650 to 750 g). A well-thought-through choice of tires can go a long way to reduce the overall weight of the bike.

Tube

Between the rim, the rim shoulder, and the tire is the tube. Tubes are usually made from butyl-plastic, and lately from latex and polyurethane. The advantage of tubes made from the latter is that they have much more resistance, and they're lighter than butyl tubes. Their disadvantages include less flexibility, and they have to be exactly matched to the tire. It's important not to expose plastic tubes to daylight, heat, and ozone rays, all of which make the plastic material porous.

Air Valve

Two different types of air valves are used for tires: the Schrader valve and the Sclaverand valve. The Schrader valve is the same as the ones used for cars and motorbikes, and they've long been used in the U.S. for bicycles. The hole in the rim that accommodates this valve must be ⅜" (8.3 mm) in diameter. The Schrader valve's advantages are that it's easier to pump air into the tires, and in the way that the valve stem is protected. A tube with such a valve stem can easily be pumped up with a hand pump or at a gas station.

A Sclaverand valve on the mountain bike is an exception. It's narrow, it needs a rim hole of ¼″ (6.2 mm), and in order to pump air into the tube, a milled nut has to be removed.

Rims

In the olden days, the mountain bike used heavy, wide, deep-bed steel rims that performed the rim's double function: to accommodate the tire, while being as strong as possible, and to serve as an important part of the brake system. Times changed when Japan (following the trend of the BMX boom) paid attention to the newcomer and produced aluminum rims for the mountain bike. At the end of the 1970s, it was possible to save 6.6 lbs (3 kg) from the weight of the bike by using these new rims.

Over time, rims became lighter and narrower.

The evolution of the rim: lighter, narrower, more aerodynamic. A good rim adds considerably to the quality of a mountain bike; it can save the bike owner a lot of trouble.

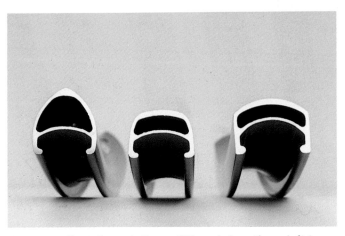

Cross sections through three different rims (from left to right): aero rim, narrow rim, and wide rim

Today the choice is not only between (30/27/23/20 mm) wide rims, but also between many different models, such as Araya, Mavic, Campagnolo, Fir, Sun, Weinmann, Rigida, Wolber, Ritchey, Specialized, Trek/Matrix and others, and a choice of tires weighing anywhere from 14 to 25 oz (400 and 700 g).

Rim Manufacturing Methods

For the mountain bike, specially shaped aluminum profiles with hollow chambers have proven very effective. They have a high degree of flexibility and resistance. "Ergal," made from an aluminum-zinc alloy, has proven to be the best material for bike rims.

Rims are made by forcing aluminum under high temperature into a profile that is cut, rolled, and welded together, or connected at the ends with metal pins (now used less often). A slightly rounded connecting piece is added for additional stability. After the hole for the valve has been drilled, the rim is anodized in an acid bath through an electrolytical process. This changes the surface tension of the material as well as its color (anodized rims are usually black or dark brown). This process makes the rim more resistant and improves the effectiveness and efficiency of the brake shoes. Stability is not increased through anodization.

Characteristics of the Rim

Aluminum rims have great advantages over steel rims: They're lighter and they're also more flexible. The material is easy to work with; under pressure it distorts before it will break. It's easy to work with even when the thickness of the walls is increased. The increased wall thickness augments the rim's stability, with only a small gain in weight. The quality of the material used determines how well a rim can be balanced. Rims behave differently when balanced. Generally, expensive, high-quality rims remain balanced much longer than less expensive, inferior rims.

The functions of the rim are: to transfer pressure from the nipple to the spoke as evenly as possible, and to prevent breakage at the joint. Less expensive rims have steel inserts to prevent nipples from breaking off. Some manufacturers, such as Campagnolo and Mavic, add small washers that help to disperse the pressure. On good rims, the holes also run in the direction of the spokes, which makes possible perfect alignment of the nipples and spokes.

The Rim as Part of the Brake System

Since the rim is considered part of the brake system, it gains added importance.

If aluminum isn't treated, the outside of the rim will soon show wear and tear from the action of the brake shoes, and from the inevitable exposure to dirt, sand, and small stones. Anodization helps prevent that damage; anodization is used by almost every rim manufacturer. Campagnolo adds a layer of chrome, making the rim even more resistant to damage. The French rim specialist, Mavic, uses a remarkable process to increase the resistance to damage even further: It adds a layer of ceramic to the outside of the rim of its latest models. Powdered porcelain is applied to the rim and treated with 20,000°C heat until the porcelain reaches a thickness of 200 microns (1 mm = 1000 microns).

This ceramic layer protects the rim from wear and tear, and most of all, it keeps the effectiveness of the brake shoes intact, regardless of weather and road/terrain conditions. If one considers the many important functions of the rim, it becomes clear that this isn't a place where one should pinch pennies. When a mountain bike isn't "made-to-order," it's important to pay attention to the quality of the rim. A good rim may save some of the trouble that lurks "just down the road." After all, the rim is *the* part that is most often exposed to danger.

Spokes

Spokes connect the rim with the hub, and they give the wheel its shape. On a good bike, enormous dynamic loads are well absorbed and distributed through flexible spokes and good rims. Good spokes (for instance, "DT Swiss") are made from a high-quality, rust-free chrome-nickel-steel alloy; their nipples are made from brass. Spokes that are strengthened at the ends are wider at the nipple and at the head than

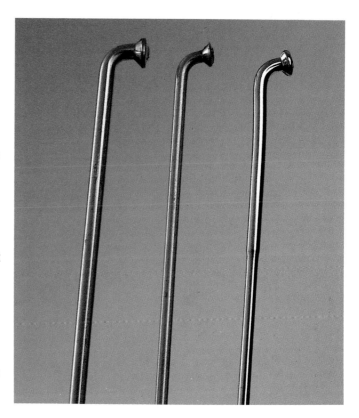

Three of the most-used spokes. Good bikes are equipped with spokes that have a different diameter in the middle than they have on the ends.

they are in the middle. Spokes for mountain bikes, however, are simple, with an even diameter over the whole length.

Spoke Characteristics

The number and diameter of spokes will depend upon the weight of the rider and the type of riding being planned. Even if it isn't obvious, spokes and nipples add considerable weight to a mountain bike. The difference between various diameters, $\frac{1}{14}''$ to $\frac{1}{10}''$ (1.8 to 2.5 mm), or different numbers of spokes (64 to 80) can make a difference of up to 27 oz (770 g). A 36-hole rim/36-spoke arrangement is considered standard for mountain bikes. Most practical are spokes with a diameter of $\frac{1}{13}''$ (2 mm), which adds up to a total weight of 20 oz (580 g) for all the spokes.

The length of the spoke is an important measurement, and the length depends upon the way the spokes are mounted, and upon the depth of the rim. Standard for mountain bikes is 3-cross spoking, where the spoke length is $10\frac{1}{2}''$ (265 mm). The advantage of 4-cross spoking is that the spokes are longer and they absorb shocks from the road surface better; the disadvantage is the additional weight.

Tightening or loosening the nipples tunes a wheel (laterally and radially), and these processes also give the spokes proper tension. Spokes with too much tension break easily at the head, under heavy loads, and with increasing age (this happens most often with an asymmetrical rear wheel). If the tension is too low, spokes might loosen while riding. The proper tension is achieved when two spokes that cross each other can only

be moved by a few millimeters. Very few bicycle manufacturers have spoking done by trained hands; in most cases a machine does this job. The spokes on new wheels of new bikes should be tightened after a few miles.

Wheel Hub

The hub determines how well a bike moves, and how much roll-resistance it has. Flanged hubs with quick-release mechanisms are used almost exclusively. No manufacturer with a good reputation will use axles with the old locknut system. The hub

Right: Four rear-axle hubs shown for comparison. Only the hub made by Sachs (top) is made for threaded rings. Below: Because of the enormous load the rear axle must carry, Campagnolo has added four ball bearings to the axle.

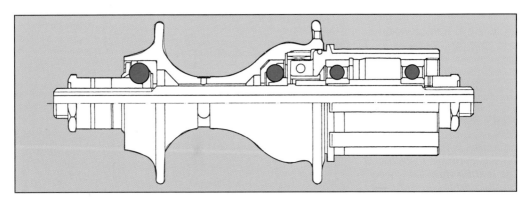

is made from an anodized aluminum alloy, consisting of an aluminum body, a bearing cup, and a hollow axle containing two or more sealed, grooved ball bearings. The quick-release mechanism allows for efficient mounting and dismounting of the wheel without using tools.

To guarantee trouble-free movement, the hub and its axle should be checked occasionally for side-to-side play. Even a small discrepancy in the distance of the ball bearings from the cone and the ball-retaining housing will cause damage and will prevent free and perfect movement of the hub.

Cassette Hub

More and more rear wheels are equipped with a cassette hub rather than with a threaded hub.

The connection of the freewheel with the wheel hub reduces the weight of the sprocket and of the hub. The space gained makes it possible to use an eight-sprocket combination.

Saddle and Saddle Post

The third place of direct contact between rider and bike (besides the pedals and the handlebars) is the saddle. This is why we give it special attention.

The saddle carries about 60% of the rider's weight and it also plays an important role in the position of the rider on his bike. The wrong saddle position can have dire consequences. For instance, an elevated saddle tip could cause inflammation of the urethra. The width of the saddle is also important: A biker with a wide pelvis requires a wider saddle; otherwise, this too can become very uncomfortable.

The best saddle designs, from a technological point of view, come from Italy, where 20 million saddles are produced every year (70% are exported). Even if the names of the saddles don't sound Italian, they still come from Italy.

A high-quality saddle is made of many different layers. Here is a cross section of a model with a gel-filled cushion.

Saddle

The supporting part of the saddle is the saddle frame (made from steel with a chrome finish, or aluminum), which is inserted into a plastic shell (for instance, those made by Rilsan). Two saddle guards, corresponding to the saddle shell, run parallel down the center and are 2″ to 3⅛″ (5 to 8 cm) long (depending upon the model). The saddle stem is attached here. The position of the saddle can be adjusted according to the mechanism provided (which is different on different models). The plastic saddle shell has an advantage in that it retains its shape while still supporting the biker's position in the saddle.

Several different materials are used for the saddle cushion: polyurethane foam covered with different types of material, like imitation leather (Skai), real leather (made from cow, calf, buffalo, snake, or crocodile hides), or gel-filled nylon/Lycra covers. The latest in technological design from Campagnolo is a leather saddle that

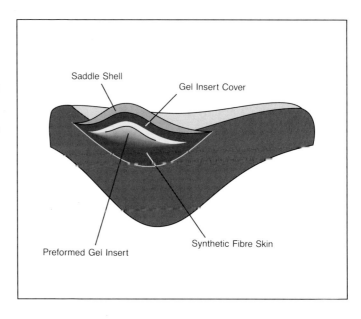

Saddle Shell

Gel Insert Cover

Preformed Gel Insert

Synthetic Fibre Skin

117

The "sportier" the bike's use, the more strength and elasticity is demanded of the saddle. A good saddle shouldn't "give" to finger pressure applied to the sides, but it should still be pliable enough to accommodate the rider's seat. A leather saddle does all this. There will be some diminished performance after 2500 to 3000 miles of riding (a few millimeters worth), but that shouldn't be bothersome if

has a removable cover under which an inflatable air bag is attached. The air bag allows for an adjustment in air pressure, affecting the degree of hardness of the saddle surface. For mountain bikes, both the leather-cushioned and the gel-cushioned saddles are equally good. Gel-filled saddles are popular because they give riding comfort right from the beginning, and they help to reduce discomfort on long trips. Leather saddles are hard and need to be broken in first. Gel-filled saddle cushions, however, have two disadvantages: First, in a crash the Lycra cover is quick to tear; Avocet solves this problem by adding a protective plastic cover. Second, the gel-filled cushions absorb rainwater faster than leather does.

Weight is also a consideration for the saddle. The Flite model is one of the lightest on the market. The seat-post clamp from Interloc is also interesting.

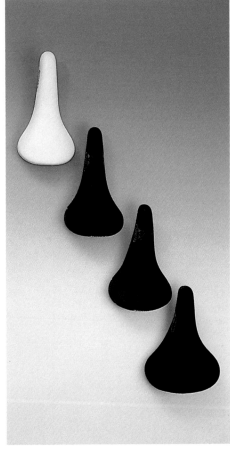

A leather saddle (white), three Lycra-covered gel-filled saddles. A saddle must be fitted to the rider's body.

the saddle fits well. In general, saddles need little maintenance.

From time to time, leather should be treated with special leather-care products, particularly after exposure to rain.

Saddle Stem

Due to angled top tubes and oversize seat tubes, seat stems for mountain bikes are longer and thicker than those used on ordinary bikes. The stems are made from CrMo steel, aluminum, or carbon-fibre. What has already been discussed in the section on tube material holds true for these stems (see page 46). However, there's no weight advantage with aluminum and carbon stems, because

the massive saddle already represents considerable weight. Furthermore, saddle stems have a wall thickness of about $\frac{1}{16}''$ (2 mm). Two aluminum clamps secure the saddle to the stem and a hex screw secures the position of the saddle. Fine-tuning of the saddle position is possible if the model has two hex screws.

It's important that the saddle-stem diameter correspond to the diameter of the saddle post. It's also important that the stem can be inserted into the saddle tube far enough, approximately $2\frac{3}{4}''$–$3\frac{1}{8}''$

(7–8 cm). Less insertion increases the pressure at the end of the seat tube enormously, and cracks in the saddle tube and distortion of the stem are not unusual.

Shimano, Suntour, Campagnolo, and Kalloy all produce saddle stems of different lengths between 11″ and $13\frac{3}{4}''$ (28 and 35 cm), and they offer stems in many different diameters in 0.2 mm increments—from 1″ to $1\frac{1}{4}''$ (26.4 to 31.6 mm). If a saddle stem has to be replaced, it isn't difficult to measure the tube diameter using callipers.

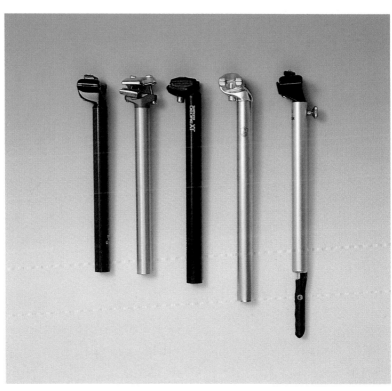

Several saddle stems. From left to right: Kalloy (made from carbon-fibre), Suntour, Shimano, Campagnolo (made from CrMo), and Odyssey (with a built-in pump)

Accessories

Computer

Bike computers are accessories that really make sense. They're made to resist any kind of weather, they're light and multifunctional. Compared to city riding, off-road riding is difficult without an accurate map to calculate distance. The bike computer will give quick answers.

"Intelligent" computers can even do more. They can give the actual speed, average speed, time of day, time distances, crank-arm revolutions, pulse rate, and more. For the serious mountain biker, the computer can calculate the gradient of descent or ascent, altitude differences, and it can note the altitude that's been reached. All of these options are programmed into computers made by Avocet and Ciclomaster.

Clothing

Mountain bike clothing should be fashionable, and it should also be highly practical. Good clothing is needed for good performance. Pants should be tight with leather-padded seats. The pants should be padded at both sides of the hips, and they should have suspenders.

The shirt, like a typical racing tricot, should be made from a breathable fibre and it should have three pockets. The best material always has been and still is wool; it's sad that this natural fibre has become scarce. Gloves and helmets are for the biker what seat belts are for the driver of a car.

Gloves protect the inside of the hands, helmets protect the head and face. Special shoes have a particular significance for the mountain biker. For the maximum transfer of power, the soles in the area of the ball of the foot should be rigid. But shoes should also be comfortable for walking and running off-road. All these demands are best served by the SPD shoe from Shimano; Look, Avocet, Time, Specialized, Sidi, and Diadora also produce good shoes.

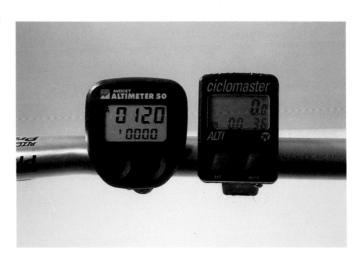

Computers with altimeters are favorites of mountain bikers.

Care and Maintenance

The mountain bike is a product of highly sophisticated engineering and, like any other vehicle, it needs attention, care, maintenance, adjustment, and repair. The right kind of care will determine the life one can expect from all of the components, and the amount of pleasure one can get from riding. One should know "how to do it" and "what to do it with." A minimum number of tools is a prerequisite.

Good tools pay back double what they cost. Adjustments and maintenance can be carried out quickly, with more precision and less energy, and parts won't get damaged when you have the proper tools.

Anyone who can perform repairs saves money and time, and he'll have more fun riding. In addition, the biker will develop an understanding of his bike's technology; he just might be able to prevent a problem even before it happens.

The oil and grease used should always be of the highest quality. Be frugal with them; too much oil and grease attract road dust. Protect the environ-ment by disposing of these lubricants wisely.

The Basics

The following should be included in a basic set of tools:
- 1 screwdriver
- 3 hexagonal allen wrenches (4, 5, 6 mm)
- Several wrenches (8–12 mm)
- 1 pair callipers
- 1 chain-rivet tool
- 2 tire irons
- Tube-and-tire-repair kit

The basic tool set shouldn't be expensive, since the tools needed for the bike are general-use tools that can be used for other purposes. All that's needed to make adjust-ments on the saddle, saddle stem, headset, handlebars, brake levers, gearshift levers, brakes, and gearshift systems, and to remove and re-place a pedal, are allen wrenches, cone wrenches, and a screwdriver. The callipers can be used to undo small dents. Re-place, shorten, or repair a chain with the chain-rivet tool. Tire irons and a tube-and-tire-repair kit are absolute musts. These shouldn't stay behind at home, they should always be stored in a pouch at-tached to the bike.

Expanded Toolbox

Those who want to do more intensive mainte-nance and repair have to reach a little deeper into their pockets: They'll need a special key for the head-set, bottom bracket, and hub cones, a sprocket re-mover, and a cable cutter. These are tools specifi-cally designed for the mountain bike, and, con-sequently, they're a bit more expensive. They're available from Campa-gnolo, Shimano, Suntour, and Var.

For those who want to take care of the "insides" of their bikes, I recom-mend a centering support, and a working stand with a working table. Problems await those who want to care for, maintain, and/or repair components made by different manufacturers. Not all tools are compati-ble with all parts.

The Most Important Tools

The tools shown in the photos on these two pages will allow one to completely take apart, care for, maintain, and repair a bike. Components such as the brakes, the

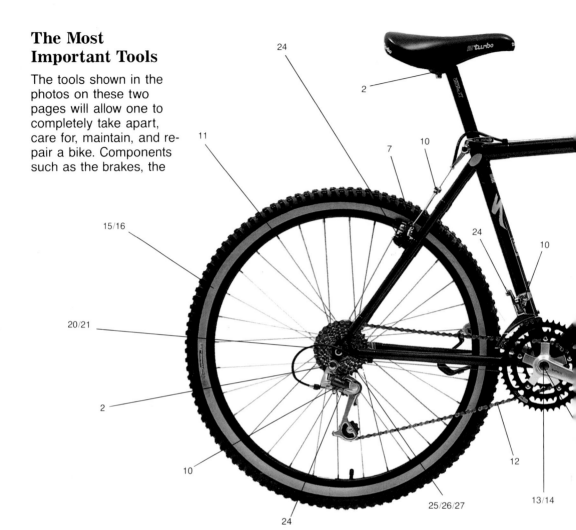

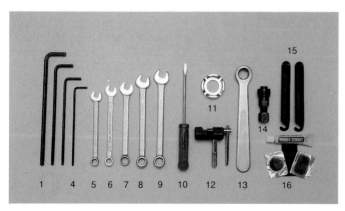

1–4 Allen wrenches (6, 5, 4, 3 mm)
5–9 Cone wrenches
10 Screwdriver
11 Centering key
12 Chain-rivet tool
13 Cotterless crank-arm wrench
14 Crank-arm puller
15 Tire irons
16 Tire-and-tube-repair kit

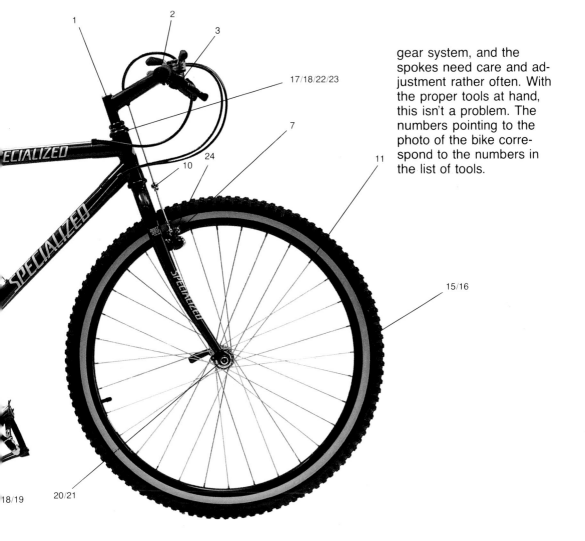

gear system, and the spokes need care and adjustment rather often. With the proper tools at hand, this isn't a problem. The numbers pointing to the photo of the bike correspond to the numbers in the list of tools.

Additional tools that are also important:
17 Headset wrench/fixed-cup, bottom bracket tool
18 Headset wrench
19 Pedal wrench
20/21 Cone wrench, counter-cone wrench
22/23 Wrenches for oversize headsets
24 Cable cutter
25 Freewheel sprocket tool
26/27 Sprocket removers

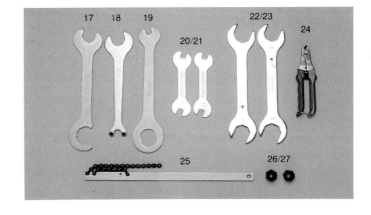

Index